Two Shadows, One Light

Two Shadows, One Light

An Inspiring Story of Brotherhood that built a Family

Authored By,

Hinali Dudhane

TLC MASTERMINDS PUBLISHING

Office Address- No. 16, 3rd Main Road, Jaganathapuram,
Velachery, Chennai 600042 (TN) India

Website: https://www.tlcpublishing.org/
Email: info.tlcpublishing@gmail.com

Published by **TLC Publishing International 2026**

Title : Two Shadows, One Light

ISBN : 978-93-6006-499-0

LIMITS OF LIABILITY/DISCLAIMER OF WARRANTY

Dedication

To my Pa and Mota Pa —

for showing me that love is strongest when it is silent,

Sacrifice is most powerful when it is unseen,

Family is the only treasure that never fades.

To my Moty Ma and Ma —

whose resilience, grace, and endless sacrifices

became the

fabric of my life.

To my Grandparents —

The roots of our family tree

taught us patience, values, and the meaning of togetherness.

To my siblings —

who walked beside me through storms and sunshine,

reminding me that even in chaos, love makes us unbreakable.

And to my whole family —

The ones who held me, healed me,

and taught me that no battle is too heavy when shoulders are shared.

This book belongs to all of you.

Foreword

By Nitin K Oza

(Ex. Vice Chairman of computer society of India-Surat and president of Surat management association)

It is a privilege to write this foreword for a book shaped with such sincerity by Ms. Hinali.

This is not merely a memoir — it is a heartbeat captured in words.

Within these pages, we witness two brothers who stood like twin pillars through illness, loss, and unimaginable odds, holding their family with courage that asked for nothing in return.

Every chapter carries warmth, truth, and a quiet strength that lingers long after reading.

This book does not just tell a story — it reminds us how love survives, how family endures.

About the Book

Two Shadows, One Light traces the emotional journey of a joint family held together by loyalty, sacrifice, and unconditional love. When tragedy struck — paralysis, illness, financial struggle, and fear — two brothers rose with a strength that shaped the destiny of nine lives.

Through real events narrated with honesty and depth, this book explores what it means to remain human when life becomes harsh. It captures the silent battles women fight within a home, the courage children learn too early, and the quiet leadership of men who never step away from their responsibilities.

This book is for anyone who has ever loved deeply, lost heavily, or held their family together with trembling hands. It is a reminder that even in the darkest chapters, one light can save everything.

Preface

This book began as a quiet promise to myself—a promise to honour two men whose strength shaped every corner of my life. My father and his elder brother, whom I lovingly call Mota Pa, carried our family through circumstances that could have broken any household. Their courage, loyalty, and unwavering sense of duty created a foundation that still guides me today.

Two Shadows, One Light is my attempt to preserve the extraordinary values I witnessed: resilience born from hardship, unity forged through loss, and compassion that never wavered, even when life demanded more than they had to give.

I did not write these pages to portray perfection, but to reveal the quiet power hidden in ordinary people—individuals who choose love over bitterness and responsibility over escape.

If this book helps even one reader rediscover hope, strength, or gratitude, then every word has fulfilled its purpose.

Prologue: The Bond that Built Me

"Some are shaped by fate. Others by faith. But the luckiest among us are shaped by love — the quiet kind, the unshakable kind, the kind that never asks to be seen, but never stops holding you together."

Parents raise some people. Circumstances raise some. I was raised by a bond — the unshakable, honest, and selfless bond between two brothers: my Pa and my Mota Pa.

They are real brothers by blood, but their relationship is something greater than biology. It is a living example of love without ego, support without expectations, and strength without ever showing off. They have never tried to be heroes — but in my eyes, they have always been just that.

I call my father Pa. And I call his elder brother, who has stood like a second father all my life, Mota Pa. Mota Pa is the elder one — calm, composed, strong like a banyan tree whose roots hold the ground firm even in the fiercest storm. Pa, the younger, is like a river — always moving, always doing, always giving, carrying with him a current of energy that never runs dry.

One rooted, one flowing. One holding steady, one carrying forward. Together, they created a bond that has shaped not only my life, but the soul of our entire family. They have taught me lessons no school or book could ever teach: how to love through actions, how to fight without breaking, and how to live with values that outlast pain.

This book is my attempt to share their journey — the story of two ordinary men with an extraordinary bond. A tale of family, sacrifice, and strength. A story that I believe the world needs to hear.

Because in a world where relationships are becoming fragile and selfishness is often rewarded, my Pa and Mota Pa remind me—and hopefully you—that real love still exists and begins at home.

So here it is — not just a story, but a heartfelt offering.

Not fiction, but a reflection of truth, love, and legacy.

A tribute to the unbreakable bond that built me.

Contents

Chapter 1

Strong Roots Don't Grow in Comfort

"Strong roots don't grow in comfort. They grow in struggle, respect, and silent strength."

Gujarat, India — a land where mornings awaken not with alarms, but with the distant echo of temple bells, where evenings descend to the rhythm of conch shells, and where the air, thick with the scent of turmeric and sandalwood, carries whispers of devotion and discipline. It was in this soil, rich not in wealth but in wisdom, that my family's story first began.

My grandparents had three sons- all kind-hearted, all raised with the same values of patience, respect and warmth. The third one, my younger uncle, is also very close to me. He carries a gentle personality, soft-spoken, charming in presence and deeply affectionate at heart. He lives separately with his family after marriage, but our relationship has always remained full of love and mutual respect. Yet, the journey I witnessed most closely- the one I grew up inside- was of My Pa and my Mota Pa, because I lived under the same roof with them. This book reflects the story I saw, felt and absorbed every single day, while still holding equal love for the one who remains a precious branch of the same family tree.

My grandfather was a man carved out of duty. He wasn't extraordinary by the world's measure — just a bank clerk with modest earnings —but in his discipline, he carried the dignity of kings. Every dawn, he buttoned his neatly ironed shirt, adjusted the strap of his worn leather bag, and mounted a rusty bicycle that squeaked at every turn. Two kilometres of road awaited him, sometimes flooded with monsoon waters, sometimes burning with the fire of Gujarat's summer. Yet he never faltered. To him, that journey was not merely to earn bread, but to honour his responsibilities.

At home, my grandmother was no less of a warrior. Her battlefield was the four walls of their small house, and her weapons were her hands — hands that kneaded dough, stitched torn shirts, embroidered dupattas for extra rupees, and held together a family with unshakable patience. She raised her sons not with luxuries, but with values sewn into the very fabric of their days. She taught them that respect wasn't spoken, it was lived; that every chore, no matter how small, was an act of love. In her house, a boy was never too important to sweep the floor, and a man was never too big to fold laundry.

Life was modest, but festivals were rich in spirit. During Diwali, earthen lamps glowed like constellations on their parapet, defying the darkness that poverty sometimes cast. Sweets were not store-bought; they were handmade Sweets, rolled with care and shared with neighbours who were more like family than friends. Uttarayan, the kite festival, turned its humble rooftop into a playground of skies. Mota Pa, calm and focused even as a boy, manoeuvred his kite with patience, while my Pa — younger, restless, and full of laughter — cheered loudly every time he cut down a rival's string.

Childhood for Pa and Mota Pa was not painted with the bright colours of toys or technology. Their joys were humble, yet unshakably profound. School mornings meant walking barefoot with chalk slates tucked under their arms, dust clinging stubbornly to their feet. If one slowed down, the other instinctively waited. They were inseparable, not just as brothers, but as shadows of each other.

Evenings often ended under the dim glow of a lantern, with their mother's voice carrying them into worlds of folk tales and moral lessons. On some nights, my Pa, playful and talkative, would interrupt with questions or jokes, making everyone laugh until their stomachs hurt. On others, Mota Pa, quiet and thoughtful, would sketch on his slate or hum a tune softly while listening, absorbing lessons with a gravity far beyond his years.

"True wealth," my grandfather often said, "is not in what you keep, but in what you can live without." And the boys lived by that truth. Their school bags were secondhand, their uniforms patched more than once, and their birthdays celebrated not with parties but with a handful of homemade sweets and whispered blessings. Yet, they never felt poor. They had each other. And in their togetherness, they were rich beyond measure.

Summers belonged to the open terraces, where the brothers would sprawl on cool stone floors, staring at the star-pierced sky, dreaming of tomorrows bigger than their today. Winters meant curling under one shared quilt, arguing over who got the warmer side, until eventually they both fell asleep, their breath rising and falling in sync.

Their laughter was their inheritance: their bond, their fortune.

Adolescence arrived quietly, like a guest who doesn't knock but makes its presence felt. For Pa and Mota Pa, it came with not just the weight of growing taller but also the invisible burden of choices that would shape their futures.

After Class 10, the world began whispering about possibilities. Mota Pa, bright and determined, dreamed of becoming an engineer. His eyes lit up whenever he saw diagrams, machines, or even the hum of a running fan. Science seemed like his path. But dreams, in those days, weren't built only on desire — they were built on affordability. Science meant extra tuition fees, expensive lab equipment, costly books, and hours that the family could not afford.

When the reality settled, he did something that only those with deep roots can do — he let go of his dream without complaint. He shifted quietly to commerce, without bitterness, without protest. That silent sacrifice, unnoticed by many, was in fact a loud declaration of his character: family before ambition, duty before desire.

Pa, the younger one, followed the same stream — not because he had no choice, but because he wanted to walk beside his brother. Where one bent, the other adjusted. Where one lost, the other held his hand tighter. Together, they redefined what education meant. It was not about prestige; it was about perseverance.

Their college days were spent on crowded buses rattling through dusty lanes of Gujarat. They often stood for hours, swaying with every brake, clutching the railings, their lunches packed tightly in steel tiffins. While other students rushed to snack stalls after lectures, they unwrapped rotis and shaak (vegetables) cooked lovingly by their mother, eating with gratitude rather than longing for what they couldn't buy.

Books were borrowed, sometimes for days, sometimes for hours. They scribbled notes furiously; afraid the owner might need the book back before they were finished. Examinations weren't just tests of memory — they were tests of endurance.

"Sacrifice is not always about giving up your share. Sometimes, it is about sharing what was never enough in the first place."

After completing their education, both brothers stepped into the world of responsibilities with the same humility they had grown up with. My Pa began working as a catering manager at a school, where he wasn't just serving meals but nourishing hundreds of children with the same care, he showed his own. And Mota Pa found his place as an accountant, his sharp mind and steady discipline becoming the backbone of the office where he worked. Neither job was glamorous, but both were dignified. They wore their roles with pride, proving that success isn't about titles — it's about integrity in what you do, and the lives you touch along the way.

And then, one day, a miracle wrapped in cement and bricks appeared: a 1BHK flat.

It wasn't grand. It had just one bedroom, a hall, and a kitchen. Cement floors that stayed cool in the summer. Windows with iron grills. Ceiling fans that hummed and buzzed like faithful companions. But for the family, it wasn't just a house — it was a milestone, a testimony to years of pedalling bicycles through rain and sun, to blouses stitched by hand, to birthdays celebrated with nothing but love.

The day they entered that flat, my grandparents didn't hold a housewarming party. Instead, my grandfather placed a small diya in the corner, its flame flickering against the pale walls, and said softly, "This light is enough. May it never go out."

Neighbours trickled in — some curious, some kind, some sceptical. But slowly, the house filled not just with family, but with trust. Festivals became brighter. On Diwali, diyas lined the balcony, glowing proudly against the sky. Holi brought bursts of colour — not bought but made at home from natural powders.

This little flat wasn't just shelter; it was a dream carved out of hardship. Every corner had a story. The narrow hallway where shoes piled up, the kitchen where aromas of turmeric and garlic clung to the walls, the small bedroom where brothers studied late into the night. It was ordinary by the world's measure, but extraordinary for those who called it home.

And beneath that roof, something deeper was being built — not of bricks and cement, but of belonging, sacrifice, and unspoken strength.

When 1997 arrived, destiny wrote a rare symmetry into our family story. My Pa and Mota Pa, real brothers, married two real sisters. In one mandap, two vows were taken; in one house, four lives intertwined. There were no lavish halls, no silver thalis lined with sweets, no camera flashes. There were only folded hands, garlands, and two couples who stepped from sacred vows into the humble reality of a shared home.

The small 1BHK flat became their kingdom. one bedroom, one kitchen, and a living space that doubled as a dining room, study, and sometimes even a sleeping area. On nights when guests stayed or when space ran out, quilts were neatly folded on the kitchen floor, and one couple would sleep there. They didn't complain. They adjusted, laughed, and took turns — making dignity their daily blanket.

My mothers entered this household not with ornaments or wealth, but with patience, humility, and resilience. Moty Ma, the elder, carried with her a natural sense of leadership. She became the silent anchor — steady, dependable, the one who always knew which bill was due and how many onions would last the week. She had a way of keeping the house afloat without raising her voice, her strength quiet but undeniable.

My own mother was younger, gentler, still growing into her responsibilities. She made mistakes in the kitchen, often learning recipes through trial and error, sometimes confusing salt for sugar in tea. The first time it happened, silence fell as everyone sipped. Then Pa, with his trademark humour, burst out laughing: "Looks like our tea is fasting today — without sweetness!" Even Mota Pa, usually strict, allowed himself a quiet smile. From that day, whenever tea tasted strange, Pa would wink and say, "So, sugar or salt today?" and the house would fill with laughter.

It was not an easy life. Money was tight. My mother began home tuition, helping children with their studies while balancing housework. She spread notebooks on the floor, teaching alphabets and arithmetic with the same sincerity with which she learned to knead dough or light the stove. For her, it wasn't just a way to earn — it was her identity, her first step into building something of her own.

Still, life inside those walls was not just sacrifice — it was stitched with stories of resilience and humour. There was the day Pa, in his absent-mindedness, placed the only house key inside the fridge next to a bowl of curd. The family searched everywhere — under mattresses, in flour tins, even inside pillowcases — until finally, someone opened the fridge, and there it was, gleaming cold on the shelf. From then on, whenever anything was lost, the running joke was, "Check the fridge first."

Festivals were perhaps the hardest test of their circumstances — and the brightest proof of their togetherness. During Diwali, with just a handful of sparklers and two rockets, both families celebrated like kings. One rocket soared beautifully into the night sky. The second tilted sideways, shooting straight into the neighbour's courtyard, landing among drying clothes. Instead of panic, Pa shouted, "Free fireworks delivery!" and laughter echoed across balconies. It became a story retold every Diwali, a reminder that the size of celebrations doesn't measure joy, but by the laughter they leave behind.

Even the discipline of the house had its moments of comedy. Mota Pa, ever the strict elder, insisted on early mornings. Pa, the night owl, would often resist. Once, after refusing to wake up despite repeated calls, he found himself drenched with a jug of cold water poured on him by his elder brother. He leapt up in shock, slipping on the wet floor, and declared dramatically, "You don't need an alarm clock if you have a Mota Pa!" From that day on, his younger cousins lovingly called him "the human alarm."

Amid these struggles and these laughs, something beautiful grew — respect. My mothers never competed; instead, they complemented one another. When one was tired, the other cooked. When one made a mistake, the other covered it with patience. They were sisters by birth, but in that 1BHK flat, they became more co-travellers in sacrifice, silent partners in keeping the family flame alive.

And at the heart of it all stood two brothers, so different yet so complete together. Mota Pa was steady, disciplined, a banyan tree whose roots gave shade and strength. Pa was cheerful, forgetful, sometimes clumsy — but he filled every corner of the home with laughter. Where one was order, the other was warmth. Where one brought direction, the other brought delight.

"Home isn't measured in square feet. It's measured in how much love can fit between its walls."

That little 1BHK, with its crowded rooms and folded quilts, was not small. It was vast, because it carried two marriages, four hearts, and the promise of a future built not on wealth, but on unity.

This was not the end of the struggle. It was only the beginning. But if the walls of that house could speak, they would whisper: Here lived two brothers, two sisters, and a bond that refused to break. Here lived love that adjusted, love that laughed, love that endured.

On Ram Navami, when the world celebrated the birth of Lord Ram, my family celebrated mine. My arrival was not just another child being born — it was a prayer answered. From the very beginning, they had longed for a daughter, and when I came into their arms, it felt as if divinity itself had touched our humble 1BHK home in Gujarat. My cradle was simple, my clothes stitched with love rather than wealth, but in their eyes, I was the most precious gift they had ever received.

Every evening, when my Pa returned home from work, no matter how tired or worn out he was, he would take me on a bike ride around our neighbourhood. That ride wasn't just a routine — it was a ritual. The wind against my face, his steady hands guiding the handle, and my small laughter echoing through the streets became a daily hymn of love. I didn't know it then, but those little rounds taught me something profound: that no matter how exhausted you are, love always finds energy.

My Mota Pa, with his quiet strength, had his own way of showing affection. In his office drawer, he always kept a bar of chocolate for me. It was never announced, never offered dramatically — but I always knew it was there, waiting for me. That one piece of sweetness carried more meaning than a thousand words. It was his silent way of saying, "You are thought of. You are remembered."

My grandparents, the gentle roots of our family tree, filled my childhood with stories. At night, when the city outside grew quiet, they would sit by me, weaving tales of courage, gods, kings, and ordinary people who rose above struggles. Those stories did more than entertain me — they shaped me. They taught me to see strength in silence, to recognise dignity in simplicity, and to believe that even in small beginnings, greatness can be born.

I was loved by everyone so much that sometimes I felt like a thread connecting every heart in that little home. And though I didn't grow up with luxury, I grew up with something richer: legacy.

"I didn't have just parents — I had pillars."

Each one of them — my Pa, my Mota Pa, and my mothers — taught me something that no textbook could hold:

- That strength can be silent.
- That love doesn't need words.
- That adjusting isn't a weakness — it's wisdom.

- That when people live for each other, miracles feel like daily routines.
- That sacrifice doesn't ask for applause — it builds something bigger than itself.
- That being different is not a weakness — it's the beauty of a family that fits together like a handmade quilt.

This was the beginning. A story that started on a bicycle. That grew in tiny flats and lived in quiet gestures. That rose without standing tall, but never stopped rising.

There were funny little moments too — like the time I cried because Pa's bike took a longer route and I thought he was lost, or when I stubbornly declared that every festival feast needed to start with chocolate from Mota Pa's drawer. My mothers would laugh at my little demands, yet still bend to them, because to them, my smile was worth more than their sleep.

And then there were moments of quiet grace — my grandmother's wrinkled hands feeding me khichdi with ghee, my grandfather holding my tiny hand as we walked to the temple, or the way they whispered blessings over my head when I slept. They were not grand gestures, but they became the foundation of my life.

Sometimes, when I sit alone today, tears still find their way without warning. Not because I am sad — but because I am overwhelmed by gratitude. Gratitude for the soil of Gujarat that held me. Gratitude for the four people who carried the weight of generations quietly, with no expectation of praise.

I was raised by hands that worked till they ached and hearts that never showed their tiredness. I didn't inherit riches or property — I inherited values, sacrifice, and a kind of togetherness this fast-moving world rarely remembers.

Everything I am today is because they never gave up on each other. Because they chose unity over ego. Because they believed in love that doesn't shout — it simply stays.

And if today I write about their strength, it is not only because they are my family. It is because their lives carry lessons the world desperately needs to learn. If strangers had walked through our humble 1BHK, they too would have left with wisdom stitched into their hearts. Because real heroes don't always stand on stages — sometimes they sit quietly at your dinner table, showing you every day what it means to love without limits.

This isn't my story. It's theirs. And now, I carry it forward — in memory, in writing, and in every heartbeat that still echoes in that little 1BHK flat.

"In a world chasing perfection, I was raised by people who chose patience. In a house with no luxuries, I lived a life rich in meaning."

And perhaps that is why this story matters — because strong roots don't grow in comfort. They grow in sacrifice, in laughter shared over scarcity, in bedtime stories whispered under lantern light, and in love that never needed an audience.

This was only the beginning.

Chapter 2

A Home Stitched with Love

"Some homes are made of bricks. Ours was built with sacrifices, stitched with love, and held strong by two brothers who chose unity over everything else."

Before the world taught me what unconditional love meant, I had already been living inside it. I did not have to search for examples in books, temples, or speeches — my home was enough. I was born into an extraordinary family, not because of wealth or privilege, but because of something far rarer: togetherness that could not be shaken.

My story has never been mine alone. It belongs to two brothers — Pa and Mota Pa — who lived not as individuals but as one heartbeat. It belongs to two sisters — Ma and Moty Ma — who mothered with equal strength, even when life tested them in different ways.

"Family is not defined by who gives birth, but by who never lets you feel alone."

Moty Ma was a quiet pillar of our home. Her story began with a wound the world could not see — a miscarriage, a silent storm that left her heart aching and her arms empty. Many women drown in grief after such a loss, but Moty Ma carried her pain with grace. She turned that emptiness into an ocean of love and poured it into me.

While my mother spent long hours guiding children through their lessons as a tuition teacher, it was Moty Ma who raised me day to day. She fed me with her hands, put me to sleep with lullabies whispered against my forehead, and celebrated my every smile as if it were a festival. Never once did she let me feel I was not hers. To the world, she was my aunt. To me, she was another mother — sometimes even my first sanctuary.

Five years later, destiny smiled on us with miracles in pairs. Both my mothers became pregnant together. That year, laughter returned to Moty Ma's eyes. She held her baby girl in her arms while my mother cradled my baby brother. Suddenly, we were three children, tied not by cousinhood but by something deeper — a bond of one soul shared across three bodies.

Our childhood was painted with the purest colours. There was no separation between whose child was whose. If one of us cried at night, both mothers rushed to comfort us. If one fell ill, both fathers sat awake by the bedside. In our home, love had no compartments, no labels, no boundaries. We were simply us —

three children, two mothers, two fathers, and our grandparents, all breathing to the same rhythm.

Mota Pa was our anchor. Every evening, he took us to the temple. It was never about rituals or complicated chants. It was about presence. Standing in that quiet courtyard, with incense rising and bells echoing softly, he taught us lessons without speaking. To be grounded. To be respectful. To show gratitude in silence. He showed us that being a father is not about gifts or grand declarations, but about consistent love that shows up every day.

"He didn't teach us prayers — he walked us into them."

Pa, on the other hand, was love in motion. His affection was louder, softer, more playful. He spoiled us with sweets, carried us on his shoulders, and said yes to every silly demand. Whether it was a balloon from a street vendor, a trip to a nearby fair, or an extra mango slice at dinner, Pa never denied us. His joy came from our happiness. In a world where fathers often guard their emotions, mine gave his freely, without hesitation, without fear.

"To the world, he was just a man. To us, he was magic. He didn't just raise us — he made our childhood feel like a dream."

Weekends were sacred in our home. No matter how tired Pa and Mota Pa were from work, Saturday and Sunday belonged to the family. Sometimes it was a stroll in the park, other times a movie in a crowded theatre where the smell of popcorn mixed with the thrill of storytelling. Occasionally, it was just sitting on a roadside bench, eating pani puri until our stomachs ached with laughter. The places didn't matter. What mattered was togetherness. Those weekends became photographs etched into memory; frames we still revisit when life feels too heavy.

Christmas was our favourite. We were not Christians, but we were believers in joy. Every year, our family dressed up in its brightest clothes and walked through streets lit with stars and bells. The smell of plum cakes and roasted nuts filled the air. We laughed, we ate, we clicked pictures under twinkling lights. For us, Christmas was never about religion — it was about family, about learning to celebrate joy wherever we found it.

"Some of the richest children are those who were loved equally — not for what they were, but for who they were."

Our grandparents were the roots that held this tree of love steady. Grandfather's discipline, Grandmother's patience, their quiet blessings — they were the background music of our lives. They did not speak much, but they showed us everything. Through their actions, they passed down values that cannot be bought in any marketplace: resilience, gratitude, and humility.

At the centre of it all were Pa and Mota Pa. Two brothers who, in a world obsessed with dividing, chose instead to unite. In today's times, families argue over money, space, and pride. But these two men shared everything — dreams, responsibilities, burdens, and joys — without keeping scores. They showed us that real brotherhood is not measured in blood alone, but in how much you are willing to carry each other's load.

"Brotherhood is not in saying, 'I am with you.' It is in proving, 'I will never let you stand alone.'"

I remember one summer when the heat was unbearable, and electricity cuts were constant. Our small flat turned into a furnace. Nights were restless, sweat sticking to our backs, fans silent in the dark. Many families around us quarrelled, frustrated with discomfort. But in our home, Pa and Mota Pa turned it into an adventure. They carried quilts to the terrace, spread them under the open sky, and told us we were camping. Fireflies blinked around us, stars glimmered above, and we drifted to sleep listening to stories of their childhood. What could have been misery became magic because they chose laughter over complaint.

"Love is not about changing circumstances. It is about changing the way you live through them."

Those summers taught me more than school ever did. That night under the stars, with three children huddled between two fathers, I understood the meaning of wealth. It was not in coins or notes. It was in belonging.

There were evenings when our tiny 1BHK felt like the world's largest stage. The three of us children would perform impromptu "shows" in the living room. A plastic stool became our stage, a dupatta tied around the shoulders turned into a costume, and the jingling of steel plates from the kitchen made the music. My brother would sing loudly, my sister tried to dance like the heroines we saw on TV, and I would narrate like a self-appointed announcer. Our audience — Pa, Mota Pa, Ma, Moty Ma, and grandparents — clapped as if we were performing in front of thousands. They didn't see our silliness; they saw our spirit.

That was the secret of our home: ordinary moments became extraordinary because they were shared.

"Joy does not need wealth to grow. It only needs people who know how to water it."

Even festivals we couldn't afford in grandeur were celebrated with the richness of unity. On Raksha Bandhan, my sister tied rakhi to both my brother and me, and then, in a rare and tender twist, we tied rakhis to grandfather. he laughed, but I still remember the softness in his eyes when we declared, "You protect us like brothers, too." In that moment, tradition was rewritten — protection was not bound by gender or ritual, it was bound by love.

Our home was not without its struggles, but every difficulty was softened by togetherness. I still remember a monsoon evening when water began to seep through the balcony. The drain was clogged, and the rain came down harder than ever. Instead of panicking, Pa and Mota Pa turned it into a family mission. With buckets, mugs, and towels, everyone pitched in — even we children, carrying little cups of water to the bathroom to pour it out. By the end, our clothes were drenched, hair sticking to our faces, but laughter bounced off the walls. The storm outside had no power over the warmth inside.

"Families that fight storms together never drown."

Sundays carried a special magic. Our mornings began with the smell of Ma's masala chai and the soft sizzle of jalebis from a nearby sweet shop. Pa would insist on buying extra, pretending it was for guests, though everyone knew it was just his excuse to indulge us. After breakfast, we'd gather on the floor with carrom. My grandfather, usually disciplined and serious, transformed into a competitive player. The thud of the striker, the cheer of a pocketed coin, the mock complaints when someone fouled — they turned our home into an arena of playful rivalry. To outsiders, these were trivial games. To us, they were lessons in patience, sportsmanship, and joy.

The temple evenings with Mota Pa continued to quietly shape us. On one particular evening, while walking back, he stopped us near a banyan tree. He placed his hand on the trunk and said, "Do you see this tree? It bends when the storm comes, but its roots hold the ground. That is how a family should be." We didn't fully understand the depth of his words then, but over the years, we saw them reflected in his actions. He bent when life demanded sacrifice, but his roots of responsibility never let us fall.

"Strength is not in standing tall. It is in knowing when to bend without breaking."

Pa, meanwhile, had a way of filling every corner of our days with humour. Once, when my brother and I refused to eat vegetables, Pa announced he had a secret recipe that would make us strong like wrestlers. He dramatically stirred the dal with a spoon as though it were a magical potion, sprinkled salt with flair, and even whispered to it like a sorcerer casting spell. When he served it, we ate it with wide eyes, believing in the magic. Years later, when I asked him why he did it, he chuckled and said, "Because feeding children takes love, not logic."

Love became our family's greatest inheritance. We learned it not from lessons but from daily practice. From the way Ma saved coins in a small steel box to buy us new clothes for Diwali. From the way Moty Ma stayed awake to finish stitching school uniforms so we could look just as polished as wealthier children. From the way Pa and Mota Pa shared one umbrella in the pouring rain rather than buy another. From the way grandparents split one sweet into seven equal parts.

"Our wealth was never stored in cupboards. It lived in our habits."

Every December, when the year came to a close, Pa had a tradition. He would gather all of us in the living room, switch off the lights, and light a single candle. In that dim glow, he'd ask us what our happiest moment of the year was. Each of us took turns answering — sometimes a new toy, sometimes a picnic, simply a day spent laughing. Pa would then say, "Remember this — happiness does not wait for big things. It lives in small sparks." That single candle in the dark taught us to notice light, even in the smallest flicker.

One winter, when money was especially tight, new blankets were out of reach. The cold seeped through cracks in the walls, biting at our toes. That night, Mota Pa quietly spread his own blanket over us children and pretended he wasn't cold. We only realised it in the middle of the night when he shivered but smiled, whispering, "As long as you sleep warm, my heart is warm too."

"Sacrifice is love's silent language. It speaks loudest when no one is watching."

Even birthdays, though simple, were unforgettable. There were no cakes with layers of cream, no balloons crowding the ceiling.

Instead, Ma baked halwa in a steel plate, stuck a single candle in the middle, and everyone sang with unpolished voices but shining faces. Sometimes the candle went out before the song ended, and Pa would relight it with a matchstick, insisting, "We don't stop until the song is done." That halwa, that candle, those voices — they were sweeter than any grand celebration could ever be.

As children, we didn't realise the magnitude of what we were being given. We only knew that every day felt full, even when the cupboards were not. Looking back, I see it clearly: our family was writing lessons into us, line by line, sacrifice by sacrifice, joy by joy.

"Our childhood was proof that you don't need the world to give you everything. You only need a family that gives itself to you."

School days brought their own stories, small yet unforgettable. Our mornings were often a comedy of chaos. Three children getting ready in a one-bedroom house was no easy task. There were endless battles over combs, socks, and water bottles. One of us would always forget homework, another would misplace the geometry box, and Pa would end up running behind us with tiffin boxes, shouting, "At least take the food, or the teacher will scold me too!" By the time we left, the entire neighbourhood knew our routine through the noise of our laughter.

But despite the rush, our parents and grandparents never let us leave without blessings. Moty Ma would put a small dot of kumkum on our foreheads, whispering, "Go shine, my stars." My grandmother slipped a spoon of sugar and curd into our mouths on exam days, and Pa, with a grin, would say, "Don't worry about marks. Just make sure your heart is honest." That line stayed with me forever — marks fade, but honesty builds lives.

"Children don't just remember what you teach them. They remember how you make them feel safe while learning."

Our grandparents were quite sculptors of our character. My grandfather never raised his voice, but his discipline spoke louder than words. At sharp 6 a.m., he rang the small brass bell kept on the temple shelf. That sound wasn't just a call to prayer — it was a reminder of routine, of order, of beginning the day with gratitude. My grandmother's stories at night carried more morals than any textbook. She told us about kings who lost kingdoms because of arrogance, about farmers who found joy in sharing, about gods who tested patience before giving blessings. As children, we were mesmerised. As adults, we realised she had been etching values into our hearts with every story.

Then there were the festivals. On Uttarayan (an Indian festival), the sky became our playground. Kites in every colour dotted the heavens, but the one that mattered most was the one flown from our terrace. Mota Pa's hands were steady on the spool, his eyes sharp, while Pa shouted encouragement so loudly the entire lane heard. We, children, ran around, gathering fallen kites, screaming in triumph every time our kite cut another. In those moments, victory wasn't just about kites — it was about knowing that even the smallest wins could feel like the world when celebrated together.

"Happiness is not in how high your kite flies, but in who stands beside you holding the spool."

Not every day was festive. Some days carried the heavy silence of worries children couldn't understand. Bills piled up, unexpected expenses arose, and dreams were often postponed. But Pa and Mota Pa never let those storms reach us. If money was short, they cut down their own needs — not ours. If tensions rose, they dissolved them with laughter before they reached the dinner table. That was their silent gift: protecting our innocence, even when their own shoulders carried weight.

"Parents who shield their children from pain give them a childhood. Parents who teach them how to face it give them a life."

One evening, I remember Pa coming home late, his shirt drenched in sweat, his eyes tired. Yet the moment he entered, my little brother jumped on him, asking for a cycle ride. Without a second's pause, Pa washed his face, lifted him onto the bicycle, and pedalled around the neighbourhood. Watching from the window, I realised something — love is not measured by how much energy you have left, but by how much you are still willing to give.

Our unity wasn't just inside the walls of our flat — it travelled with us. On weekends, we went to fairs where the smell of roasted corn filled the air, where toy sellers shouted with full lungs, and where children's laughter rose above the noise of the crowd. We never bought much, but every outing was treated like a festival.

Even eating one ice cream cone passed around among three kids became a celebration.

And then came winters, when the nights grew colder, and the power cuts more frequent. Instead of complaining, Pa taught us shadow games on the wall with a flicker of candlelight. Rabbits, birds, and strange creatures danced in the glow as our laughter filled the room. Mota Pa quietly watched, smiling, before adding his own creation — a shadow of folded palms that looked like a lotus. That lotus became our family symbol: blooming even in the darkest night.

"Love does not remove darkness. It teaches you to bloom within it."

Looking back now, I realise we were never just living days — we were writing chapters of resilience, humour, and faith. Every small act was a lesson disguised as play. Every shared meal was a story of sacrifice hidden in routine. Every laugh was a defiance of hardship.

And as I write these memories, I can still feel it — the way our tiny 1BHK pulsed like a single heartbeat. It was crowded, yes, but never suffocating. It was small in size, but vast in spirit.

Perhaps that is why, when I step out into today's world and see families breaking over ego, pride, or money, my heart aches. Because I know — I lived inside a miracle many people only dream of. A miracle named family.

"This chapter isn't just my memory. It is a mirror held up to a world that has forgotten what real family means."

As years passed, the walls of our home held countless stories — some written in laughter, some in tears, and many in silence. But no matter what the world demanded, our family never forgot the one truth that bound us: love comes first.

I often think of the children we were — three little souls who never once felt the absence of anything. Not because we had everything, but because we had everyone.

"Some families break because they count what they give. Ours lasted because they counted only what they shared."

Even today, when I close my eyes, I can hear the echo of temple bells that Mota Pa led us to, feel the tickle of Pa's laughter as he spoiled us, and see the patient smiles of Ma and Moty Ma working quietly in the background. I can smell my grandmother's hand-ground spices, hear my grandfather's bicycle creak as he returned home, and picture three children curled under one quilt, breathing in rhythm.

If sacrifice had a sound, it would be the quiet hum of our nights.

If togetherness had a heartbeat, it would be Pa and Mota Pa.

"This chapter is not nostalgia. It is a reminder that the simplest homes can teach the grandest lessons."

Because somewhere out there, a family is fighting over land, over inheritance, over pride. Somewhere, children are growing up in separate rooms, never knowing what it means to fight over one blanket. Somewhere, laughter has been replaced by silence. To them, I want to say — love is not found in bigger houses or larger bank balances. It is built in small acts, in shared struggles, in choosing unity when division feels easier.

My childhood was my greatest blessing, not because it was perfect, but because it was real. And reality, when woven with sacrifice and love, becomes legacy.

"Legacies are not built in monuments. They are built in meals shared, in burdens carried, in hands held through storms."

And so, Chapter 2 closes not as a memory but as a message:

That is when two brothers choose to live as one, when two sisters stand as partners in sacrifice, when grandparents become the roots and children the blossoms — then a family becomes unshakable.

It is not a fairy tale. It is not fiction. It is what I lived.

And it is what I hope the world remembers — before it is too late.

And so, let me end this chapter with a poem — a prayer, really, for every family searching for its heartbeat again:

Not built of stone, not built of gold,

Our home was a story silently told.

A roof of sacrifice, walls of care,

A love so endless, it filled the air.

Hands that worked, yet never complained,

Hearts that gave, though nothing remained.

Two brothers, one bond, stronger than steel,

Two sisters who taught us what wounds can heal.

Laughter in scarcity, hope in despair,

A candle of joy in shadows we'd share.

Three children who grew not apart, but as one,

Under the gaze of the moon and the blessing of the sun.

So if the world forgets, let my story remind:

True riches are not what you leave behind.

It is love — quiet, stubborn, endlessly true,

That builds a family and rebuilds you.

Chapter 3

When Separation Hurts More Than the Storm

"Nature can test your strength. Life can shake your foundation. But a family rooted in love will always find its way back to each other."

Every family has a moment when love must move from words into proof. For us, that moment arrived in 2006, when the skies over Surat city darkened not just with rain but with a test that would leave its mark on us forever.

The rain began as a whisper against the windows. Children like us celebrated it, pressing our palms against cool glass, watching droplets race each other down in crooked lines. We cheered when the first puddles formed outside, splashing barefoot until Ma called us in with mock scolding. At first, it was fun. Rain always felt like freedom.

But by the third day, freedom turned into fear. The river swelled, refusing to stay within its banks. Streets disappeared beneath angry waves. Electricity failed, plunging neighbourhoods into a darkness broken only by the flicker of candles. Radios crackled with warnings, but none of us could have imagined the scale of what was coming.

By the time the water surged into our building, it was too late. The ground floor vanished. Then the second. By the time it reached ours, Pa and Mota Pa exchanged one long look — a look that said everything without words. Without hesitation, they gathered us all. With grandparents trembling, children clinging, and two mothers balancing fear with strength, we climbed flight after flight until the terrace opened above us like the only safe sky left.

We carried little — a few clothes, a stove, rice and lentils sealed in tins, and the kind of courage you don't plan for but discover in moments like these.

And then began ten long days.

We built a shelter from plastic sheets, tying ropes to poles and praying the wind wouldn't rip them away. Nights were wet, windy, and sleepless. Rain tapped on the plastic like an endless drumbeat. The terrace floor was hard, but we arranged mats and quilts, huddled close, our warmth becoming each other's blanket.

Food became ritual. Moty Ma cooked on a tiny stove, flames fragile against the damp air. Sometimes all we had was khichdi — thin, watery, stretched to feed nine mouths. And yet, Pa would joke, "Who needs a restaurant when we have our terrace café?" He would announce the "menu" every evening with dramatic flair —

lintel soup, rice pancakes, cloud curry. We laughed, even when hunger gnawed. Because their love never lets us feel poor.

"When the world strips you bare, family turns scarcity into celebration."

We children invented games to fight fear. We played stone-and-coin, raced paper boats across puddles on the terrace, and tried to guess cloud shapes as they passed. Every night, Pa or Mota Pa told us stories. Some were folktales, others were memories from their own childhoods. My favourite was the one Mota Pa said during a stormy night — about the baby bird they once rescued, small and broken, who never learned to fly but still became their teacher of love.

At the time, it was just a story. Years later, I realised it was a prophecy. That flood was our fallen bird — a broken moment. And yet, in nursing it together, our family discovered its own wings.

But not everything was play. There were nights when the sky roared louder than our laughter. When the wind threatened to snatch away the plastic sheet that was our only roof. On one of those nights, I remember clutching my grandmother's arm and whispering, "What if the water comes higher?" She stroked my hair and said, "Child, water may rise, but so will we. Because we are together."

"Fear loses its power when someone stronger holds your hand."

Neighbours shared the terrace with us; their faces lined with the same uncertainty. Some had lost everything. Some whispered about relatives missing. And yet, amid despair, a strange unity blossomed. One neighbour shared a candle when ours ran out. Another lent salt when we had none. Children from different families played together, forgetting divisions. Floodwaters drowned walls, but on those terraces, humanity stood tall.

When the tenth day finally dawned with silence instead of rain, it felt unreal. Slowly, water began to retreat. We walked down the steps, feet squelching on soaked stairs, into a home that no longer felt like ours. The walls were cracked. Furniture swollen. Floors smelled of rot. The house we had built with years of love had been scarred in just days.

But what none of us knew then was that the real storm wasn't the flood. It was the decision waiting in its wake — a decision that would wound us more than water ever could.

When the floodwaters finally receded, we thought the worst was over. But sometimes, the storms outside are easier than the ones inside.

Our home, like many others, had been stripped bare. Mould crept across walls like uninvited guests. Mattresses sagged with dampness. Clothes carried the smell of mud. The kitchen shelves that once held food now held silence. Everything familiar felt foreign.

That was when Pa and Mota Pa made a decision, not out of anger or pride, but out of practicality. With finances stretched thin and a home barely liveable, they thought it would be better — at least for a while — to live separately in their own houses. Perhaps they believed it was temporary. Maybe they thought it would lighten burdens. But love sometimes makes decisions that logic later regrets.

And so, for the first time in my life, our family split into two households.

At first, it seemed manageable. The mothers tried to reassure us, "It's just for a while." Our grandparents reminded us, "We are still one family." Pa and Mota Pa promised, "We'll visit every day."

But what no one realised was how deeply separation seeps — not into walls, but into hearts.

The silence was the first thing we noticed. In a joint family, silence is rare. There's always a spoon clinking in the kitchen, a child laughing, a grandfather humming a prayer, or Pa cracking a joke. But in those weeks apart, nights grew eerily quiet.

My brother and sister suffered the most. They were in the same class, and every day at school, they clung to each other like vines, unable to let go. Teachers often had to separate them, but the real heartbreak came after school. The moment they saw each other at the gate, tears spilled. They hugged tightly, refusing to move, as if afraid that walking away meant losing each other forever. Even adults could not watch without tears in their eyes.

"Some bonds are not built on bloodlines alone. They are stitched by shared mornings, laughter at the dinner table, and silent hugs after bad days."

At home, the mothers carried double burdens. My Ma tried to keep her tuition classes running, but she had a hollowness in her eyes, glancing often at the empty chair where Moty Ma used to sit while helping with chores. And Moty Ma — she took even more. She had her daughter to raise, but she also made sure we were cared for when we visited. She never complained, but I saw her wiping tears when she thought no one was watching.

Our grandparents tried to hide their pain, but age has no disguise for grief. My grandfather's hands trembled more as he read the newspaper alone, without Pa and Mota Pa sitting beside him. My grandmother cooked smaller portions, setting fewer plates on the floor, her sighs hidden beneath the clang of utensils. For people who had spent decades holding their family like prayer beads, every bead now felt missing.

The hardest part was the festivals. Diwali came, but the diyas glowed dimmer. Without both families lighting lamps together, the house looked incomplete, shadows stretching farther than the flames. Birthdays felt less like celebrations and more like reminders of what was missing. Even Christmas, our favourite, became a quiet outing rather than the lively parade of lights and laughter we once knew.

"Separation does not always mean fighting. Sometimes it is simply a silence that eats away at joy."

I remember one evening when the sky was painted orange with sunset, and my little sister tugged at my hand. She whispered, "Why can't we just go back? Even if it's small, even if it's crowded, at least it feels like us." Her words pierced deeper than any adult explanation ever could. Because she spoke the truth — children don't care about comfort, they care about closeness.

One night, unable to sleep, I overheard Pa and Ma whispering. Pa said softly, "I thought this would make it easier. Instead, I feel like half of me is missing." His voice cracked — a sound I had never heard before. Ma reached for his hand in the dark, but neither of them had answers.

"Love is not always loud. Sometimes it is the sound of a father whispering regret in the dark."

Days turned into weeks. Weeks turned into months—seven long months of pretending. On the outside, we tried to smile. On the inside, we were wilting.

And then, one evening, the silence broke.

My sister returned from school, eyes red, clutching her tiny books. She had cried again. She had cried too many times. That night, Mota Pa sat silently in the corner, watching her sleep. His face was firm, but his eyes softened. Then, with the kind of certainty that comes only once in a lifetime, he turned to Pa and said:

"This isn't who we are. Let's stop pretending that two houses can hold one soul. We built a life together — we must live it together. Even if it's tight, we will make space. But we will not let love divide us anymore."

And Pa, without hesitation, nodded. No arguments. No ego. Just relief.

"Sometimes, true strength lies not in enduring separation but in choosing reunion — even when it's hard."

That night, the decision was made. We would come back.

The very next week, our family moved back into Mota Pa's 2BHK. It wasn't a grand event. No trucks lined the street, no helpers carried furniture. It was just us — arms full of bags, hearts full of anticipation.

I still remember my grandfather folding bedsheets with trembling hands, whispering, "Now it feels like home again." My grandmother lit a diya in the corner, tears glistening in her eyes as she placed thalis for all of us once more. The sound of utensils clinking, children laughing, and elders calling from one room to another — it was the music our house had been missing.

"You don't measure the size of a home by square feet — you measure it by the number of hearts willing to share it."

Yes, the house was tight. Two bedrooms were now stretched to the limit of what comfort allowed. Closets were crammed, and quilts had to be spread on the floor at night. Privacy became rare. Yet what we gained was priceless: wholeness.

Our evenings came alive again. Pa resumed his routine of taking us out, sometimes to a small park, sometimes just for a walk around the neighbourhood. Mota Pa brought us to the temple, his steady presence restoring discipline to our days. Festivals bloomed again with light and laughter. Even birthdays — still celebrated with halwa and a single candle — felt radiant.

But the reunion wasn't just about children laughing or grandparents smiling. It was about healing wounds that separation had carved.

I noticed it first in my brother and sister. Their tears after school slowly stopped. Instead of clinging in desperation, they ran home with joy, knowing the distance between them had vanished. They studied together again, shared snacks from the same plate, argued over pencils, and fell asleep side by side. Their innocence, once bruised, began to glow again.

Ma and Moty Ma also softened. The weight in their eyes lifted. I saw them working together again — cooking side by side, sharing stories, even laughing at small mistakes. The quiet strength of their sisterhood returned, stronger than before.

And Pa and Mota Pa? They were once again the pillars, different yet inseparable. Pa, with his warmth and humour, continued to spoil us — sneaking in our favourite snacks, staying up late when one of us couldn't sleep, fulfilling small wishes before we even voiced them. Mota Pa, steady as always, became our compass, guiding without words, teaching us that consistency is the deepest form of love.

Together, they were more than just fathers. They were lighthouses — one glowing with laughter, the other with direction — both guiding us safely to shore.

"Strength is not only in facing storms. It is in choosing, again and again, to keep walking side by side."

Neighbours often asked how we managed in such a small space with so many people. They couldn't understand why we gave up comfort for chaos. But what they called chaos, we called family. What they called compromise, we called love.

Because in that crowded little flat, there was no loneliness. Every corner hummed with belonging. Shared hands softened every struggle. Every celebration, no matter how small, became grand because we had each other.

"Luxury is not space. Luxury is unity."

I often think back to the terrace during the flood. The plastic roof that kept us dry, the tiny stove that fed us, the laughter that carried us through fear — all of it was possible because we were together. And the separation that followed taught us the same truth in reverse: when we are apart, even comfort feels empty.

The flood tried to drown us. Separation wanted to divide us. But nothing was strong enough to break the bond of two brothers who refused to let go of each other, who chose reunion over pride, who

believed that family was worth every sacrifice.

"Family doesn't fail when it breaks. It fails only when it forgets how to return."

And so, we returned — stronger, softer, closer. Our journey carried cracks, but those cracks became our character. Our home became more than walls and windows — it became proof that storms may come, separations may happen, but love always finds its way back.

To this day, when I think of that chapter of our lives, tears rise uninvited, not because of the pain, but because of the grace. We lived through fear, separation, longing — and yet we came out holding each other tighter. That is the kind of wealth no flood can wash away.

And if I could whisper one truth to the world, it would be this:

"When separation hurts more than the storm, you know it's time to come home."

The flood came to test, the storm to divide,

But love held us firm, side by side.

Water can drown, and silence can sting,

But unity rebuilds what loss cannot bring.

Two homes apart left our hearts torn,

Nights grew colder, days felt worn.

Yet through the cracks, a light broke through,

A bond unbroken, a love so true.

Back we came, into one embrace,

Crowded rooms, but endless grace.

Tight was the space, yet vast was the heart,

For no distance can keep true souls apart.

So if you wonder what makes a home,

It isn't walls or space to roam.

It is love that refuses to drift away —

It is the family that chooses to stay.

Chapter 4

"Broken, not Defeated"

"Some days don't begin with a sunrise…they begin with a scream you never forget."

It was a morning like any other, simple, quiet, routine. My father left home early to work, riding his familiar two-wheeler. He had done it a thousand times before. That day, the sun rose just the same, the birds sang just the same, and we went on with our lives just the same… unaware that by that evening, everything we called normal would be torn pieces.

But that morning was not just any morning — it was Ganesh Chaturthi, 7th September 2014. While the city of Surat prepared to welcome the remover of obstacles, our own home was about to be struck by the greatest obstacle of all. The sound of drums in the distance, the chants of "Ganpati Bappa Morya," were drowned in our lives by a soundless scream that destiny had written for us.

In the late afternoon, the phone rang.

It wasn't Pa.

It wasn't someone who knew us.

It was a stranger – a nurse from the emergency department of the government hospital. Her voice was professional, but there was something in it that cracked open hearts. "This number was found in the wallet of a man brought to the emergency ward. He's in critical condition. Please come here immediately."

That wallet- the small brown one we had seen Pa carry in his shirt pocket for years- had become the only clue to his identity. Now, it lay beside a man drenched in blood, mud, and silence.

We didn't wait a second.

We left everything behind and rushed. Our feet moved fast, but the world around us felt like it had slowed. The city outside was still buzzing, but inside us, a storm had begun.

The hospital was chaos- people crying, nurses shouting, stretchers rolling across dim corridors. We ran to the emergency room, and when we finally saw him…we shattered.

My Pa lay there, unrecognisable.

His clothes were soiled in blood and canal water. Mud clung to his hands. His body trembled, still fighting for his life. His face was pale. His eyes closed. Breathing, but barely.

For a moment, I refused to believe it was him. My mind screamed, "This cannot be my father." But then I saw his hands. The same hands that once carried me on bicycle rides are now lifeless and cold. The same shirt pocket where he kept toffees for me, now soaked in blood. Nothing prepares you for seeing your hero broken.

We later found out what had happened.

A reckless car had hit him at full speed and fled, without so much as a glance back. His vehicle was tossed aside like it meant nothing. The collision was brutal- the kind of impact that silences the world in an instant. Pa's body was hurled into a roadside canal, where muddy water swallowed him halfway, and silence wrapped itself around his pain.

For nearly five hours, he lay in that canal — motionless, unseen, unheard. Imagine this: Ganesh idols being carried with music through the city, people dancing in celebration, and in the same city, my father bleeding silently in dirty water, unseen by hundreds who passed. Humanity failed that day, but destiny held on to him.

For nearly five hours, he lay there- not moving, not speaking, not even conscious. His body was broken, bones fractured, spine damaged, blood speeding into the earth beneath him. The water around him slowly turned red, but the world rushed on as if nothing had happened.

People passed by slowly moving vehicles. Life moved- but nobody saw him.

That day, humanity failed him, but fate didn't. Somehow, even with fractured bones and shattered breath, his heart kept beating- stubbornly, softly- refusing to give up.

Then…finally. Mercy arrived in the form of a stranger. A young boy, perhaps sent by fate itself, spotted the barely visible shape in the water. Something made him pause. Maybe it was intuition, maybe it was a whisper from the universe. He stepped closer, and what he saw changed everything. Without wasting a second, he called for help.

That boy became the bridge between life and death. To this day, I believe he was not just a passerby — he was an angel in human form. If he had ignored the sight, if he had walked away, I would not be writing this chapter.

An ambulance arrived. And with it, a new battle began.

When we saw him, we couldn't breathe. My mother's legs gave out. My grandparents clutched each other, whispering prayers. My siblings and I stood still, too shocked to cry. He had always been our protector. And now he looked like a wounded child, helpless and broken.

The doctors worked quickly.

The injuries were grave. There was internal bleeding, a head injury, and his spine had cracked. He was paralysed from the waist down. "The next 24 hours will decide everything", the doctor said. "We've done all we can. Now, it's up to him."

Those words were knives. How do you wait for 24 hours, knowing every second could be the last? The hospital clock became an enemy, every tick louder than thunder.

So we waited.

We waited, like people holding on to the edge of a cliff. We prayed with desperation. Every beep of the monitor felt like the rhythm of hope. My mother sat outside the ICU with folded hands, whispering his name over and over. My grandparents lit lamps at home and refused to eat until he opened his eyes.

"Sometimes, love is not loud. It's a whisper repeated in prayers, over and over, until the universe listens."

And finally...the universe did.

Pa survived.

But he did not wake up whole.

The accident had taken more than just his ability to walk. It had taken our peace. It had stolen our certainty. It had paused life as we knew it. We had entered a new reality- one filled with hospitals, therapies, medicines, and unknowns.

And for almost two years, he could barely move his neck. Imagine lying flat, day after day, unable to even turn to see the people you love. That was his prison, and yet he endured it.

And yet... in the middle of all that pain, something extraordinary rose.

Mota Pa.

He didn't just step in; he became our pillar, our shelter, our strength. Quietly, without needing to be asked, he stood beside his brother like a shadow that would never leave.

"Real strength is not lifting weight.... but in lifting people when they can't stand on their own."

When Pa opened his eyes again, something in him was different. Not just his body, his voice, his gaze, even his silence felt heavier. The stitches on his head were deep. His spine had suffered serious damage. And the worst part…he couldn't move his legs.

The doctor called it partial paralysis. They explained things: signals, nerves, and spine compression. We heard none of it. All we saw was the man who once carried us on his shoulders, now lying still, unable to lift even his feet.

In those early days, he asked once in a cracked whisper, "Will I ever dance with you again?" None of us dared to answer. The silence was heavier than the truth.

My Mota Pa didn't say much. He didn't cry loudly or make a big declaration. But every single night, he was there in the hospital. He'd bring extra clothes and sit silently next to the bed. Wipe Papa's forehead when it's sweating from the pain. Hold a spoon to his lips when he was too tired to eat. Watch monitors, we were too afraid to look.

No one asked him. No one needed to. He just showed up for four straight months.

I once saw him fold Pa's blanket so gently, like it was something scared. I asked him if he was tired, and he just smiled: "What else would I do? He is my brother."

Even the nurses whispered about him. "That man with kind eyes," one of them called him. They saw it too- that rare, rare love.

I remember one night that broke something inside me… and rebuilt something stronger. It was sometime in the second month. The hospital had become our second home- the cold benches, the antiseptic smell, the silent prayers whispered into folded hands. That night, around 3 am, Pa's BPDU began to convulse. The machines beeped an alarm. My mother rushed to call the nurse. I stood frozen. But my Mota Pa… he didn't flinch. He gripped Pa's hand tightly and leaned in, whispering in his ear like he was speaking to a sleeping child. "Raju… I'm here. You're not alone. Just breathe."

The nurse came running and injected something into the IV. Slowly, the tremors stopped. But Mota Pa didn't let go of that hand, not for the rest of the night.

Around dawn, I saw him walk out of the ICU for just a few minutes. I followed him, quietly. I found him in the dim corridor, slumped against the wall, face buried in his hands. That was the only time I ever saw him cry. Silent tears, no sobbing, no noise. Just pain that had been swallowed for weeks, finally rising like a tide.

When he saw me, he quickly wiped his face and straightened up. "I am okay." He said. But I was not. I wasn't okay watching the strongest man I knew carry a storm in his chest.

That was the night I truly understood what love looks like when it's stripped of words- raw, tired, aching love that still shows up, still chooses, still stays.

The quiet backbone:

He never raised his voice to speak,

Yet held the strong when we were weak,

no need for words, no grand display-

His silence lit the darkest day.

each evening came, he found his place,

a gentle strength, a steady grace.

no clock, no claims, no waiting cue-

He simply came, as love would do.

No one assigned him such a role,

He chose it, stitched it into his soul,

nine hearts he bore with no complaint,

a saintly strength, though not a saint.

It wasn't blood that drew the line-

but something deeper, more divine,

the kind of bond that time can't sever,

Two brothers, one soul, bound forever.

People say blood makes a family. But this was something more. This was a man choosing, every single day, to carry the burden of nine hearts on his shoulder- without ever calling it a burden.

When Pa finally returned home, it wasn't like a celebration. It wasn't a happy ending. It was a quiet, painful beginning of something we had never imagined- a life we didn't prepare for.

We brought him home not in a wheelchair, but in an ambulance- flat on a stretcher, surrounded by silence and fear. He couldn't move, couldn't turn, couldn't even lift his neck because of the cracks in his spine. The man who once stood like a mountain was now carried in like glass.

For almost two years, Pa could not move his neck at all. He would stare at the ceiling endlessly, unable to turn even towards the voices calling his name. Imagine the cruelty of wanting to look at your children but not being able to shift even an inch. Every day became an exercise in patience, in waiting for someone to adjust his pillow, tilt his head, or simply hold a mirror so he could see the world. Those two years felt like decades.

As the ambulance halted at the building entrance, our entire society stood outside. Some with prayers on their lips, others with hands folded silently. No one said a word- because no one knew what to say. Many of them had seen him earlier jogging, playing cricket, and doing workouts. That was who Pa had always been- stronger, generous, larger than life.

He had been a gym enthusiast for years. His discipline was unshakable. Muscular, confident, fit like only film heroes- he was the kind of man who didn't just lift weights, he lifted spirits. People admire his energy. Children waved at him when he returned from his morning run. Even at home, he was our strength- physically, emotionally, in every possible way.

And now... his muscles had softened. His chest barely rose with breath. His once-proud posture now lay flat and dependent.

There's no silence heavier than the one that surrounds a man brought home broken.

Our strong Pa- who once danced with us in the living room- now had to be lifted by people just to sit up. His bed was placed in the middle of the living room, near the window. Not because there was no space, but because that's where we could keep an eye on him, talk to him, keep him close.

That bed became the centre of our universe. It was no longer just a piece of furniture; it was the battlefield where we fought every day to keep hope alive. The smell of medicines mixed with incense sticks, the sound of the monitor replacing the sound of his laughter, and yet, that little corner of the room became the most sacred place in our house.

The house wasn't big. My grandparents were in one room. The rest of us- me, my siblings, my mom, Mota Pa - adjusted however we could. But Mota Pa never let us feel like we were inconveniencing anyone. Not once. He simply made space- in the house, in his heart, in his daily routine.

We had no income. My Father, the only earning member on our side, was now bedridden. My mother had to leave her job to become Pa's full-time caregiver. She had never spent a day without her job... and now, she was learning to lift his body, clean his wounds, schedule medications, and most painfully- wipe his tears.

But Moty Ma stepped in without being asked. She cooked every meal with dietary care. She would sit beside Pa during his feeding hours and whisper, "Don't lose hope." Sometimes she'd cry while washing his bed sheets stained from bed sores, but she never let us see defeat in her eyes.

There were nights when I woke up thirsty and saw lights in the kitchen. It was always her- warming food, making something light for my mom, preparing soft meals for my Pa's morning routine. She became a bridge between pain and healing. And Mota Pa - he became the pillar that didn't shake even in a storm that cracked every wall we had built.

He paid for our school fees, Pa's endless medical bills, the medicines, physiotherapy, tests, and travel, and never once said, "I can't." Never once did he make us feel like we were taking too much.

He just gave.

And gave.

And kept giving.

In those years, Pa also endured more than ten surgeries to treat his unrelenting bedsores. Each surgery felt like reopening wounds that had barely begun to heal. We prayed every time he was taken into the operating theatre. Sometimes the surgeries worked, sometimes the wounds returned worse than before. It was a cycle of pain, but Pa bore it all without asking, "Why me?" He simply whispered, "Let's try again."

One evening, I overheard a relative asking him, "How are you managing all this?"

He smiled - the same tired but gentle smile he always wore- and said, "God gave me two hands, one is for working. The other is for holding my brother."

Even now, years later, I don't think I have heard a purer definition of love.

And in the middle of all this... Two small souls were growing up too fast.

My brother and sister were only ten. Children by age - but warriors by heart. They weren't taught how to be brave. Life demanded it.

One day, when Pa couldn't eat, it was my brother who stepped forward with a small bowl of rice. His hands trembled, but he said, "Pa, I will feed you today." he climbed onto the edge of the bed and tried to feed with his small hands. It was clumsy- the spoon shook, some of it spilt- but Pa opened his mouth anyway. Maybe not out of hunger, but out of love.

No one asked my brother to do it. No one taught him how. But somewhere, deep inside that little boy, he had understood something adults often forget- when someone you love falls, you don't wait to be told what to do. You just show up.

And my sister- she would sit beside the bed, quietly watching Pa sleep. One evening, I heard her whisper to the ceiling fan, "please god, fix him. I will be good forever. promise." She never said much to us. But she told everything to the sky.

These children had once played doctor with toy stethoscopes. Now, they stood by a real hospital bed, learning real courage.

And still, MotaPa never once let the weight show.

He went to work.

He fixed leaky taps.

He argued with chemists to reduce medicine bills.

He hugged us quietly on days we broke down. And every time the lights went out metaphorically or literally, he was the one who found the switch again.

"True courage isn't loud. It's found in small acts of love that keep the world from falling apart."

The days turned into months, and Pa's body became a map of scars and survival. The bedsores were brutal, deep, painful, and unrelenting; some wounds took weeks to heal, and others kept returning like a cruel reminder of how fragile life had become. At times, we had to call doctors twice a day. The living room turned into a makeshift hospital, and yet, not once did Pa ask for pity.

I still remember the way he cried- not loud, but quiet.... silent tears slipping down his face as the doctors changed his bandages. he bit his lips to stop the sounds, not for himself, but so we wouldn't hear. He didn't want to become our sorrow. And somehow, even in his suffering, he was still trying to protect us.

We tried everything- from expensive physiotherapy sessions to homemade ayurvedic oils that filled the air with a scent of hope. Someone even called a spiritual healer once. He placed his hands gently on Pa's knees and whispered prayers, as if his touch could restart the nerves that had gone numb.

But it was also during this phase that something else began — something we still hesitate to speak about. In the hospital, Pa would whisper in a trembling voice, "I feel like someone is sitting near me." At times, he said it felt as if unseen hands were dragging him, trying to pull him away. Anklets that no one wore echoed faintly in the corridors. We never told outsiders, but within the family, we knew something beyond science walked those nights with us. Perhaps one day, this story will unfold in its own book. For now, it remains a shadowy memory locked inside this chapter.

"Will I ever walk again?" Pa once asked, eyes clouded with quiet desperation.

And in that moment, silence filled the room. The kind of silence that doesn't comfort- it suffocates.

But Mota Pa, as always, stepped forward and answered with a voice that felt like a promise:" You will. Maybe not today, not tomorrow... but until then, we will walk for you."

And he did.

For years, Mota Pa walked every step Pa couldn't. Hospital visits, medicine pickups, school meetings, bank queues, grocery runs- all for a brother who had once walked tall, but now lay in one place.

"Love doesn't always look like grand gestures. Sometimes, it looks like walking silently beside someone who can no longer move."

My mother- she left her job, her identity, her independence. But she never once showed regret. She learned to read prescriptions, clean surgical wounds, lift a full-grown man with trembling arms, and most importantly- hold his spirit together when it threatened to break. Her love was fierce, but silent. Tireless, but never demanding.

There were mornings when her hands shook from fatigue, yet the tea never spilled. There were nights when her back screamed for rest, yet she kept turning him gently, hour after hour, to ease the pain of the wounds. If strength had a face, it would look like a mother refusing to let despair cross the doorway.

My Moty Ma never let my mother walk alone. She cooked every meal with care, made sure Pa's food met the doctor's guidelines, and quietly wept as she scrubbed bloodstains from the bedsheets.

She hid her tears in the running tap, letting the water carry them away. And when she returned to Pa's bedside, her eyes were dry again — because in our house, hope learned to stand up, even after it fell.

Our family blurred all definitions. There were no 'your children' and 'our children'. There was just 'us'. We sat around the same table, wept in the same room, and prayed with the same breath.

That single breath — shared across nine hearts — became our anthem. When one of us broke, another hummed the tune. When one of us forgot the words, another sang louder.

And then came the question we had all avoided for months. "How long can we survive like this?"

The hospital bills were growing like wildfire. Our savings had melted. My father's strength was gone, and so was our income.

My mother had left her work. And though the house was filled with love, it echoed with silent fears- how would we feed nine people, run a household, and continue my father's treatment?

It is frightening how fast numbers can crush a soul — bills, dues, medicine slips — but that fear never learned the language of our home. In our house, fear met faith, and faith learned to work.

One morning, with trembling lips and an unshaken spirit, Pa looked at me and said, "We'll start our catering business again. I can't move... but I can still manage. I'll guide you through everything. And this time, we'll name it after you- "Hinali Caterer."

He was still, but his dream wasn't. We had stopped the catering work for a full two years after the accident — the vessels slept, the ladles fell silent — and yet, from his bed, he lit the stove again. (We began calling it "Hinali Caterers," but he never cared for names — he cared for feeding people right.)

That name- my home- became a new kind of responsibility. A symbol of the legacy he wanted to build, even from a bed.

I said the name out loud — once, twice — and felt my spine straighten. It wasn't just a business. It was a promise stitched to my own breath.

We didn't cook ourselves- we had a team. Old chefs who had worked with us once came back without asking for advances. Some refused the pay until we stood on our feet again. Loyalty returned like a full circle. Even suppliers allowed us credit. That was the power of my Pa's goodwill. He couldn't stand, but his values stood tall.

When the first sack of rice arrived on credit, I touched it like prasad. Every lentil looked like a prayer someone had answered.

The first order under "Hinali Caterer" was small - a birthday for 25 people. But for us, it was like being handed the contract for a royal wedding. My father lay on his bed, giving instructions, deciding menus, balancing costs, and suggesting garnishes. The staff stood around him like students before a master.

He corrected the salt by memory, not by taste. He set the timing by instinct, not by clock. He arranged the sequence of dishes the way a poet arranges lines — so that the last bite completes the first.

And I?

I was no longer a child. I was the front face of his dreams. The voice to his silence. The hands to his wisdom.

I learned to read a client's face the way doctors read scans — anxiety, hurry, pride, doubt — and serve not only food, but reassurance.

That birthday order turned into another, then another. Slowly, like a dry river filling with rain, hope returned.

Hope did not roar back. It arrived like steam rising from fresh dal — quietly, invisibly, but filling the room with warmth.

No, it wasn't easy. There were days we made losses. Days we didn't sleep. Days we got scolded by clients and still smiled. But every single plate we served meant a little more life for Pa.

We weren't running a catering business; we were running on

courage. We were surviving on faith.

"When your back is against the wall, you don't wait for a miracle- you become one."

I remember one evening clearly. The lights had gone out in the whole area. It was humid, chaotic. Our catering team had to prepare food for 150people in that heat. My brother, barely 10, was helping carry boxes. My sister was folding paper napkins and sealing boxes. And my father constantly called us, "Check the salt in the curry. That family likes it light."

Even paralysed, he remembered the client's taste. That was the level of detail he gave.

When the generator finally coughed to life, and the first tray left our door, I felt something inside me return — not luck, not money — dignity.

And that night, when the guests appreciated the food, my father's eyes welled up. He couldn't attend, he couldn't move, but he was there in every flavour.

"Strength isn't measured by what your body can carry, but by what your heart refuses to let go."

That business didn't make us rich, but it gave us back our dignity, our rhythm, our belief. It reminded the world- and us-that we weren't defeated.

"Sometimes, healing doesn't come through medicine.

It comes through movement, purposes, and faith stitched together by love."

We didn't just restart a business. We restarted life.

And while life returned, the shadows sometimes did too. On a few nights, as he lay awake, Pa whispered that he felt a presence by his side — not cruel, not kind, just watching. We never chased the mystery; we guarded the man. If those shadows have a story, we will tell it another day.

If there is one thing this chapter of our lives taught me, it's this- you don't need perfect conditions to rise. You don't need everything to fall into place. You just need a reason. And we had one, our father, our family, our survival.

People often wait for the storm to pass. But sometimes, life demands that you learn to dance in the rain. That you open your broken fists and still offer something to the world- even when you feel you have nothing left.

We weren't trained for business. We didn't have capital or contacts. But we had something far greater- a reason to fight, a reason to wake up, a reason to keep going, and sometimes, that's all it takes.

"Success isn't born in comfort. It grows in crisis, watered by courage, and lit by the fire of purposes."

When your life shatters, you have two choices: let the pieces cut you... or use them to build something new. We chose the second.

To anyone reading this- struggling, stuck, or silently suffering- know this:

You don't have to have it all figured out. You don't need to take giant leaps. Just take one honest step. Do one honest thing. Cook one meal. Send one email. Show up for one person. That's how you rebuild.

"Rock bottom is not the end, it's the foundation. And you, even broken, are enough to build again."

Because sometimes, the most successful journeys begin not with confidence... but with courage whispered through tears.

We rebuilt belief.

We rewrote what love can do.

And above all, we stood, even when everything tried to keep us down.

Pa's condition remained fragile, but the spark in his eyes was back. Maybe couldn't walk, but he could sit and smile at us, tell stories, and crack the same old jokes.

And when he smiled, it felt like a window opened. Fresh air entered. The house remembered laughter.

We didn't count profit in rupees anymore- we counted them in recoveries, in full meals, in laughter that slowly returned to the living room. The home that once echoed with silence now hummed with quiet hope again.

Sometimes I caught my Pa staring at MotaPa- not with words, but with the kind of gratitude that speaks from the soul.

One night, I saw them sitting together. The TV was on, but neither of them was watching. My Pa whispered something, and Mota Pa simply placed a hand on his shoulder.

No one said "Thank You. " No one had to.

Because in the language of real love, some things are understood in silence.

My Mota Pa didn't sleep well for months. He didn't buy new clothes for himself. He gave up his own comforts so the rest of us could feel some. He fed nine people, clothed nine hearts, and never once made us feel like we owed him something.

He just kept saying, "We're together, that's enough."

And truly, it was.

If I ever forget what grace looks like, I will remember this sentence. It fed us more than bread. It covered us better than blankets.

At just sixteen, I was forced to mature beyond my years. While my friends spoke of movies and school trips, I was calculating medicine costs and grocery bills, watching my father's chest rise slowly at night just to make sure he was still breathing. My childhood didn't end; it transformed. I was no longer just a teenager. I became a quiet warrior, holding our pain.

"Some kindness cannot be returned- they must be remembered."

Even now, when we gather as a family, we still sit close. I still eat from shared plates. Still look out for one another, just as our parents once did in silence and sacrifice.

Our childhood was interrupted, yes. But it was gifted- with the rarest kind of education: compassion in action, love without conditions, and loyalty that asks for nothing in return.

"Sometimes, life bends you so far, you think you'll break. but in those moments, you find out what you're really made of- and who's truly standing with you." We were scared. But never broken.

And at the core of it all were Pa and MotaPa- two brothers bound not just by blood, but by a promise to never let go of each other, no matter what came their way.

They showed us that family isn't about shared DNA- it's about shared tears, shared burdens, shared victories, and silent prayers whispered in the dark.

They reminded the world of a truth many forget:

"You don't need riches to be royal- you just need a heart big enough to carry the weight of others."

As I close this chapter, I know one thing with certainty:

I may never be able to repay what MotaPa did for us. But I will live my life in a way that honours it.

And when the day comes that I am asked, "How did you learn what family means?" I will smile - and say:

"I watched two brothers love each other through the worst storm in their lives. And that love became our shelter."

And if you ask me what a miracle looks like, I will not point at the sky. I will point at our living room — one bed, two brothers, three children, four hands cooking, and a house that learned to breathe again. That is where God chose to live with us.

Chapter 5

One More Battle

"Some storms come quietly, without thunder or lightning. They slip into your life like a shadow, and before you know it, the air you breathe feels heavier, and the ground beneath your feet begins to shake."

We thought we had seen enough storms. After Pa's accident in 2014, after the long months of hospitals, prayers, and sacrifices, we believed nothing could wound us more deeply. We were already scarred, already tested, already holding on to faith like a rope in a flood. But life had one more test waiting — a test that didn't knock at the door but slipped silently into our home.

I remember it clearly — the fear didn't begin with screams this time. It began with silence. With a mother who smiled through pain, who cooked meals while her own body was fighting a hidden war. With whispers in the kitchen, with half-finished sentences that we children weren't supposed to hear. With a lump no one wanted to believe could mean more than a swelling.

When life tries to shatter a family that's already endured more than most, it's not just pain that returns — it's fear. And in 2016, two years after Pa's accident, we met fear again. This time, wearing a white coat and holding a scan report.

Moty Ma had a small lump in her breast. At first, she ignored it — as mothers often do, placing everyone else's needs above their own. She kept cooking, cleaning, smiling, carrying on as if nothing had changed. But her body had begun whispering truths she couldn't hide anymore. When the pain grew louder than her tolerance, she agreed to see a doctor. The tests came back. The lump wasn't just a lump. It was a tumour. The news came like a second storm over a house that still hadn't rebuilt its roof from the last one.

At first, the doctor said surgery would be enough. Remove the tumour, and it would be fine. We clung to that hope like a drowning man clings to driftwood. But midway through the operation, the doctor called Mota Pa into the hallway. I wasn't there, but I have imagined that moment a thousand times — the hospital's bright white walls, the smell of antiseptic, the weight of unexpected decisions.

"The tumour is malignant," the doctor said, "it's cancer. We need to remove the entire breast."

Mota Pa stood silent for a second. And then, without panic, without delay, he signed the papers.

A signature that didn't just authorise surgery — it carried grief, fear, protection, and the weight of love that doesn't ask questions.

That day, Mota Pa didn't just save a life. He proved, once again, what it means to carry a family on your shoulders — even when those shoulders have been bearing weight for decades without rest.

Moty Ma came home post-surgery — fragile, stitched, bandaged. And that's when reality truly began.

We now had two patients. My father, still paralysed, still healing from a broken spine, still confined to his bed in the living room — and now Moty Ma, with postoperative weakness, limited movement, and a body learning to accept its new form.

Our house had always been small, but now it felt even smaller, not because of space, but because every corner carried the weight of suffering. The smell of medicines hung in the air, mixing with the faint scent of turmeric and cumin from the kitchen. Pill packets lay scattered on the dining table, bedsheets were folded and unfolded endlessly, bearing the stains of pain and the signs of survival. Our 2BHK was no longer a home — it was a battlefield, and each of us had our own post to guard.

Our small 2-BHK apartment became a recovery ward. There was no nurse. No full-time helper. Only family.

My mother became the quiet warrior once again — bathing both patients in bed every morning. First Pa, then Moty Ma. She never showed exhaustion, but I saw it in her eyes — the kind of tiredness that doesn't sleep, just survives.

Her hands, once used for writing tuition and teaching children the alphabet, now lifted heavy bodies, sponged wounds, and adjusted IV tubes. Her lap was no longer a place of comfort for us, but a place where she gathered the strength to cry silently when no one else could see.

We, three children, were growing in years, but life pushed us far beyond our years. I was sixteen then, but I felt thirty. My brother and sister were barely twelve — still meant to be chasing kites and doing homework — and yet I saw them carrying towels, adjusting pillows, feeding Pa spoonful of rice when mom's hands were full. One morning, I saw my twelve-year-old brother lifting Pa's head gently and wiping his mouth with tissues. He didn't flinch. He didn't complain. He didn't even look for praise.

Because in our house, kindness wasn't taught. It was absorbed — like sunlight through a window you didn't even know was open.

My sister, too, grew into her courage silently. She would sit beside Moty Ma, combing her hair carefully so she wouldn't feel the loss of her breast alone. One day, she even tucked flowers into her braid and whispered, "You are still beautiful." Those words, spoken by a child, carried more healing than any medicine.

And Mota Pa?

He was the gravity that held us in place.

He arranged for the medicines. He took care of the medical appointments. He listened when we were too broken to speak. He stood with folded hands beside Pa's bed and whispered prayers every night.

He never once asked, "Why us?"

He simply said, "We'll manage."

And manage, we did. Through sleepless nights and endless bills. Through cracked ceilings and thinning bank accounts. Through fear, pain, and fatigue that clung to our skin like dust.

Sometimes, nights were the hardest. The ceiling fan whirred above, the street dogs barked outside, but inside, the silence was heavy with unspoken fear. We, children, pretended to sleep, but we could hear our mothers moving from one bed to another, adjusting, comforting, whispering prayers under their breath. Those nights taught us that true courage doesn't come with loud voices — it comes with quiet endurance.

Moty Ma, even in her pain, tried to stay cheerful. "At least, I still have one hand to cook," she joked once, while making a light dinner for Pa and herself. Her face was pale, her eyes tired, but her spirit — uncrushed.

Sometimes, she'd sit next to Pa's bed with her own bandaged chest and say, "If we've come this far, we'll go further," and he would nod because they were more than in-laws. They were siblings in suffering. Two souls bound by years of sacrifice and shared strength.

"True courage is when broken people still offer a hand to help others rise."

The house felt never silent anymore — not because there was noise, but because hope had found its way back in, in the aroma of slow-cooked food. In the dim lights that stayed on late. In the way we looked at one another, not as separate families, but as one beating heart.

There was no space for selfishness in that house. Only room for grace.

Relatives came, one after another — mother's sisters, cousins, extended family we hadn't spoken to in years. But no one came empty-handed. Someone brought fruits. Someone brought snacks. Someone stayed the night so my brother could get a few hours of sleep. In moments like these, you learn what "family" really means — it's not the ones who visit during festivals. It's the ones who show up when all the lights have gone out.

Some nights, our living room looked like a waiting room — plastic chairs lined up, thermos flasks of tea being passed, and whispers of prayers that never stopped. Even when people couldn't give money, they gave their time, their presence. And sometimes, that was worth more than gold.

One of my relatives arranged for discounted physiotherapy sessions. My mother's sister sat with Moty Ma, combing her hair, keeping her company while she winced through the pain of healing. These weren't just visits — they were lifelines.

They reminded me of something I will never forget:

"Blood may connect you by birth. But love connects you by choice. And that kind of bond is unbreakable."

Even in this storm, school was never skipped. Homework was still done. Meals were still made. Clothes were still folded. Not perfectly, maybe, but lovingly. My younger sister once stayed up all night making handmade cards for both patients, because she said, "they need something happy."

That morning, when Pa woke up, he found a paper star taped to the wall above him that read: "You are my hero." Next to him, Moty Ma's bedside table had a card with shaky glitter writing: "Mom, you are stronger than pain." Those fragile pieces of paper carried a strength that even medicines couldn't provide.

That night, our living room was decorated with paper stars, a cake made of biscuits, and candles stuck into a bowl of rice. There were no guests, no music, just claps, laughter, and eyes that filled silently when no one was looking.

We didn't need a party. We had each other.

I remember standing at the door that night, watching from a little distance. For the first time in months, I heard laughter that wasn't forced. Pa smiled faintly, Moty Ma tried to clap with one hand, and my grandparents' faces glowed in the candlelight. It wasn't a grand celebration — but it was proof that even in brokenness, joy finds a way to sneak in.

Sometimes, I'd stand in the bathroom window at night and whisper to the stars, "Please make things better." Not because I didn't believe in doctors, but because when everything is broken, faith is the glue you hold on to.

"When the world gives you nothing, give each other everything."

One day, I caught Pa smiling as he watched Mota Pa fix a broken chair. His body was still weak, but his spirit was full. He said, barely audible, "he is my legs now."

And he was.

That one sentence has never left me. It was not just a line; it was a vow. Pa could not stand, but he had someone who stood for him. It taught me that sometimes life takes away abilities, but it never takes away love — unless you let it.

When a family breaks up, people often drift. But not us. We pulled tighter.

When people asked me today what strength looks like, I pointed back to that house — where two patients were healing, three children were growing, and a family was quietly writing the most powerful story I've ever known.

"In the deepest valleys of life, you discover the tallest mountain within your soul."

Even as a teenager, I stopped asking for things most kids did — new clothes, birthday parties, outings. I had grown into a silent observer, learning life's hardest lessons not from textbooks, but from tired hands, whispered prayers, and nights lit by more hope than lamps.

"Some of us grow up when life doesn't give us a choice. But that doesn't mean we grew up empty — it means we grew up full of grace."

I learned to measure life not in years, but in responsibilities carried. At sixteen, while others spoke of dreams, I spoke of medical bills. While my friends worried about exams, I worried about whether Pa's medicines would arrive on time. That childhood was stolen — but in return, life handed me an education in resilience no university could offer.

My Mota Pa was tired.

Even when he was scared.

Even when there was nothing left to give, he gave more.

Sometimes I think of him as the unseen author of our survival — writing chapter after chapter of sacrifice without ever holding a pen. His handwriting was on every bill paid, every meal served, every quiet moment when he stood strong while the rest of us crumbled.

We owe him everything. And no, I can never pay him back — but I can carry his values forward.

To every relative who stood beside us, to every cousin who held a hand, to every sister who wiped tears without needing to be asked — thank you. You didn't just help us survive; you reminded us what true love is made of.

And to the world, I say this:

You don't need palaces to be rich.

You don't need money to be powerful.

You just need love — in its rawest, most unfiltered form.

Because love, when it stands in the middle of disaster, becomes a miracle no one saw coming.

"Greater isn't about what you build — it's about what you keep standing, long after everything has fallen."

And yet, there was something else — something we rarely spoke of. Nights when silence felt too heavy. Nights when Pa whispered, he felt shadows near his bed, as though unseen hands tugged at him, trying to take him away. We never shared this with the world. We wrapped it in prayers, in threads, in the soft glow of a diya. To some, these things may sound like fear. To us, they were a reminder: when life walks close to death, the line between the two becomes very thin. One day, perhaps, this story will demand its own book. For now, it rests in the unspoken corners of our memory — half mystery, half truth.

And through it all, I watched two brothers — Pa and Mota Pa — carry their family like warriors. Quiet, loyal, undefeated.

They taught us that pain can bend you, but it can not break you — not when you hold each other up.

They taught us that life is not about what happens to you, but how you respond when it does.

And most of all, they taught us this:

"Strength isn't proven by what you conquer — it's proven by how you keep walking forward, even when the road beneath you has already collapsed."

Chapter 6

Quarantined, but Never Alone

When the world went quiet, our home became the loudest it had ever been — not with noise, but with meaning. In 2020, when the word "lockdown" became a universal sentence, we found ourselves enclosed within the four walls of our small home — not as prisoners, but as one undivided family. Nine people in one home.

COVID-19 changed everything — from how we breathed to how we believed.

Outside, the world was filled with fear. News channels screamed numbers. Masks became mandatory, and distance became law. Sirens replaced traffic. Hospitals overflowed. Doors shut tight. But inside our home — something opened.

We didn't have extra space or luxury, but we had something rare: togetherness. In a time when isolation was the global norm, we lived each day wrapped in each other's presence. The same floor, the same ceiling, the same meals — but nine different souls leaning on each other like never before.

Only one person stepped out — Mota Pa.

He was the only one permitted to leave the house because he was working for a company that built COVID isolation cabins. Even in those terrifying months, when most people feared stepping outside for milk or medicine, Mota Pa wore his mask, took his bag, and left before sunrise — not for adventure, but for duty.

He didn't just bring home his salary. He brought home courage. He carried back not only groceries and medicines, but also the assurance that, even in a world of uncertainty, we were not abandoned.

Each evening, when the main door clicked open, we all paused — listening for his steps, waiting to hear that familiar, calming voice. Sometimes he entered with tired shoulders, his face marked by the straps of his mask. But even then, he smiled.

He smiled not because life was easy, but because he didn't want us to feel how hard it was.

"Some men wear uniforms to serve the world. Some just wear responsibility — and never take it off."

That was Mota Pa. He never stopped showing up — not when the city drowned in flood, not when Pa fell into a canal, not when Moty Ma battled cancer, and not now, during a global pandemic.

And the rest of us? We were finally together, every minute of every day. And somehow, amidst all that chaos, we began to heal in ways we didn't know were needed.

We watched one movie every evening — a new ritual that became our escape. It didn't matter if it was an old black-and-white classic, a silly comedy, or a film we had already seen three times. For those two hours, the heaviness outside melted away. We sat close, sometimes with blankets on the floor, sometimes with plates of homemade popcorn. The screen flickered, the fan creaked above, and our laughter bounced off walls that had once echoed with worry.

One night, while watching a thriller, my younger brother kept covering his eyes with a pillow. My grandfather, instead of comforting him, started adding his own sound effects — making ghostly noises until we all laughed so hard the neighbours could probably hear us through the walls. Even fear became comedy in our home.

My sister and I experimented in the kitchen — trying recipes we had only seen on YouTube until then. Some turned out surprisingly good. Some ended up burnt in the pans and too salty, but no one complained. We laughed through our mistakes and served them anyway.

Once, we tried making cake in a pressure cooker. We forgot to add baking powder, and it turned into something harder than a cricket ball. My grandfather jokingly suggested we keep it for self-defence, while my grandmother said, "At least it smells like cake!" That became our family joke for weeks — whenever something went wrong, we called it a 'pressure-cooker cake.'

Even our grandparents joined in the experiments. They would sprinkle extra spices on top, but that was the magic — we weren't feeding mouths, we were feeding memories.

We played Ludo nearly every day. A simple board game — four tokens, one dice — but for us, it became a battlefield of love. My younger siblings fought over turns. We teased, we argued, we teased again. And beneath it all — we bonded.

One evening, the game got so heated that my little sister stormed away, saying she'd never play again. Ten minutes later, she returned quietly, placed her token back on the board, and muttered, "I'll only play one round." Of course, she stayed for three hours. That's how love works in families — anger doesn't last longer than the sound of dice rolling.

The news outside told stories of loss, but inside our four walls, we created stories of survival.

"When everything around you falls apart, build something that can't be seen — a bond, a memory, a moment."

We built all three.

One evening, during our usual movie hour, the electricity went out. The fan stopped. The room turned warm and silent. But instead of frustration, someone lit a candle. We all sat in that dim light, cross-legged, as my grandfather began telling old stories — of his childhood, of war, of life before mobile phones. For a moment, it felt like time had paused. No pandemic. No lockdown.

Just three generations breathing under one roof — listening, learning, loving.

That night, my grandmother added a song to his stories — a soft, old devotional tune. Soon, my mother hummed along, my sister joined with her thin but sweet voice, and even Pa tapped the bed rhythmically with his fingers. Our little 2BHK flat became a concert hall of broken voices, but to us, it was more beautiful than anything playing on TV.

In those hours, I realised something: the world was teaching us fear. But our home was teaching us faith.

Faith in simplicity. In shared meals. In board games and bad recipes. In showing up. In holding on.

And most of all — faith in one another.

Even as we built joy inside our small home, grief still found its way to our doorstep. COVID did not spare anyone, not even the strongest souls. My mother and Moty Ma lost their father — our maternal grandfather — during the pandemic.

He had always been a towering figure in their lives. A man of discipline, humility, and warmth, he carried wisdom in his silence and love in his simple gestures. For us grandchildren, he was a storyteller and a guide. For his daughters, he was the first man they ever looked up to.

When the news of his passing reached us, it felt unreal. There was no last hug. No proper farewell. Just a phone call, a few broken words, and silence that stretched across the room like a shadow.

We couldn't even gather together as a big family to grieve, because restrictions didn't allow it. Funerals became numbers, rituals were shortened, and traditions were interrupted. My mother sat quietly in the corner, holding her dupatta to her face, weeping silently so that Pa wouldn't see. Moty Ma pressed her palm against her chest, whispering prayers to a father she couldn't go near.

For the first time, I saw the two women who had always been our pillars of strength, bend under the weight of sorrow.

But even in that storm, they carried us.

Pa was already paralysed. He couldn't attend the rituals, couldn't walk into the gathering, couldn't even offer his shoulder to his wife in her grief. Yet he tried in the only way he could — whispering words of courage, reminding us that their father would want them to stay strong. His voice trembled, but his intent was steady.

That's when I learned something profound:

"Sometimes the ones who need the most comforting end up comforting others."

In those days, we all became caregivers in small ways. My siblings took over the household chores, so Ma wouldn't feel overburdened.

I remember one night, my younger brother tiptoed into the kitchen and quietly made tea for Ma. The sugar was too much, the taste a little off, but when she drank it, she smiled through her tears and said, "It's perfect." Because in grief, it isn't about the tea — it's about the love that boils with it.

Moty Ma, even with her own fragile health after cancer, stayed close to Ma. They sat together late into the night, sometimes talking, sometimes not. Just sitting. Because grief doesn't always need words — it needs presence.

That period of loss taught us that families don't heal by running away from pain. They heal by carrying it together.

"When sorrow becomes too heavy for one pair of shoulders, that's when family lifts it as one."

We couldn't change what happened. We couldn't bring him back. But we honoured him by protecting each other even more fiercely.

And though the world outside kept showing us numbers, to us, that one life lost was not a statistic. It was love. It was a memory. It was family.

After losing our grandfather, grief became a quiet guest in our home. It didn't shout, it didn't rage — it simply sat in the corners, waiting for moments when silence grew too loud. And yet, in the same breath, we had to continue with life.

Our father was already paralysed, unable to move his neck for nearly two years after the accident. His condition demanded constant attention — medicines, physiotherapy, careful feeding, and endless care. My mother and Moty Ma carried that responsibility like seasoned warriors, even as their hearts were bleeding from the loss of their father during COVID.

I understood that true resilience is not about moving mountains — it is about folding laundry with tears in your eyes, cooking a simple meal with trembling hands, and still smiling when your children look at you.

We, children, stepped in wherever we could. My brother took charge of sanitising the groceries and checking off the lists Ma made. My sister made it her mission to keep Pa entertained. She'd sit beside him with her schoolbooks, reading aloud not because he asked her to, but because she thought maybe the sound of her voice would distract him from his pain.

I took care of the digital side of life — online bills, virtual updates with relatives, and making sure Ma didn't have to run outside for every small need. It was a strange mix: being a teenager while handling responsibilities that felt far beyond my years.

But perhaps that's what life was teaching me:

"Maturity doesn't come with birthdays. It comes with battles you never expected to fight."

Even the smallest tasks carried weight.

One evening, Pa whispered that he wanted his pillow adjusted just so, because his neck pain was unbearable. I spent nearly half an hour getting it right — folding, refolding, sliding towels underneath, watching his face soften when it finally gave him relief. That tiny smile felt like the biggest victory of the day.

Another night, the lightbulb in the living room fused. It was just a bulb, something ordinary, but to us it was crucial — because that was the room where Pa stayed. My brother climbed up on a chair, carefully fixing it, while Ma held the chair steady and Pa watched silently. When the bulb lit up again, the whole house clapped as if we had just restored electricity to the entire city.

It was these little victories that kept us moving.

And then, there were moments of unexpected laughter — the kind that reminded us we were still alive.

One afternoon, my sister tried making food. They turned out saltless. Pa, watching her struggle, teased her gently: "If you serve these, the guests will run away before eating." She laughed so hard she dropped the rolling pin. That laughter echoed louder than the grief in the room.

We realised something important then:

"Joy doesn't arrive when life is perfect. It arrives in imperfect kitchens, in burnt rotis, in mismatched routines — when love is bigger than sorrow."

Grief has a strange way of testing people. Some break apart. Some close their doors. And then there are families like ours — who, even while mourning, somehow find ways to create life inside the cracks of loss.

After losing my maternal grandfather, my mother and Moty Ma never let their sorrow overshadow their duty. They had tears in their eyes, yes, but their hands never stopped working. The kitchen fires never went out. The medicines were never missed. Pa's physiotherapy was never skipped.

It was as if they were telling us silently:

"Pain can pause your heart, but it should never pause your responsibilities."

We, children, learned to notice the smallest details. If Pa's water bottle was half empty, we refilled it before he asked for it. If Moty Ma shifted uncomfortably, my sister rushed to bring her a cushion. If the sanitiser bottle ran low, my brother refilled it from the larger container. These weren't grand acts, but each one said: "We're paying attention, we're here, you're not alone."

There were days when grief would hit suddenly, like a wave. Once, while cooking, Ma broke down silently, tears falling into the dough she was kneading. I watched from the doorway, unsure whether to step forward. Before I could, Moty Ma walked over, placed her hand on Ma's shoulder, and whispered, "Don't worry, I'll take over. Go rest." It wasn't just about cooking. It was about carrying each other's sorrow without words.

In those moments, I realised that true love between family members isn't loud — it's quiet substitutions, gentle handovers, unspoken relief.

But grief didn't only bring silence. Sometimes, it brought strange, almost unexplainable experiences.

One afternoon, I found Moty Ma sitting quietly by the window, staring out at the street. I sat beside her. After a long silence, she said, "Do you know, your Nana always told me — storms don't ask permission before coming. But they also don't last forever." Her voice trembled, but her words anchored me.

Pa too had his silent battles. Nearly two years after the accident, his neck still refused to move. He couldn't turn to see who entered the room. Every time we walked in, he only knew us by our voices. Yet, he never stopped asking about us. "How was your day? Did you eat? Did you finish your homework?" His own body betrayed him, but his heart still reached out to us.

It was in these moments that I realised something profound: Paralysis may chain the body, but it can never imprison the spirit.

And then there were the nights — those eerie nights that still linger in memory. Sometimes, Pa whispered that he felt as though someone was pulling him, dragging him into an unseen place. We never dismissed him. Instead, we sat closer, whispered prayers louder, and lit more candles. There are things science can't explain, and perhaps never will. For us, those moments weren't just about fear — they were reminders that life is fragile, that we were fighting battles both seen and unseen.

"Some shadows are not meant to be explained. They are meant to remind us of the light we must protect."

But in between these shadows, there was light too.

We made birthdays special even in lockdown. No bakeries were open, so my sister crushed biscuits, mixed them with cocoa, and pressed them into a cake mould. She decorated it with gems and wrote "Happy Birthday" with white cream. It was messy, but beautiful. When we cut it, Pa's eyes glistened. It wasn't about the cake. It was about the fact that even in crisis, we refused to stop celebrating life.

Sometimes, the best defiance against pain is joy. And we chose joy.

When days turned into weeks and weeks blurred into months, the lockdown taught us something no classroom ever could: life is not measured by what happens outside your walls, but by how you choose to live inside them.

I remember one particular day. Pa's bedsores had worsened, and he needed urgent dressing. The nurses couldn't come because of COVID restrictions. My mother stood by his side, trembling hands holding the cotton and antiseptic. She cried quietly as she worked, whispering apologies to him as though she had caused his pain. And Pa, lying there with his head still immobile, whispered back, "Don't cry. You are my strength. If you break, I will break."

That single sentence held us all together.

The small victories that reminded us why we kept fighting. The day Pa managed to move a single finger after weeks. The day Moty Ma laughed loudly at a silly joke, the scar on her chest was visible, but her spirit was unbroken. The day all nine of us sat on the floor, eating dinner from one big plate, because the gas cylinder had run out, and yet, somehow, that meal tasted like the best feast of our lives.

It was in those moments — fragile, fleeting, yet unforgettable — that we realised something profound: even in lockdown, we were not trapped. We were held. By each other. By love. By faith.

As the months of lockdown slowly loosened their grip on the world, people stepped outside again. Roads filled with cars. Markets buzzed with noise. Schools began talking about reopening. Life, in fragments, returned.

But inside our home, something had already changed forever.

We were not the same nine people who had entered that lockdown. We had walked through fire together. We had carried grief, laughter, fear, and faith all in the same breath. We had lost — deeply, painfully — our maternal grandfather, a man of dignity and kindness. His absence left an empty chair in our hearts that no one else could fill. And yet, even in his absence, he left us one final lesson: that a good man's influence never dies. It lives on in the love of his children and grandchildren.

Our mothers carried his teachings forward. Their resilience, their sacrifices, and their silent tears turned into the roots of our strength. Watching them, every woman reading this should know: you are stronger than you think. You are capable of carrying storms and still offering shelter. You are the quiet architects of survival.

Every child in the house carried something forward, too. My brother learned responsibility years ahead of his time. My sister learned compassion in ways her peers couldn't imagine. I learned that life doesn't pause for you to prepare — it demands you to rise, whether you're ready or not.

And Mota Pa? He became more than just the backbone. He became the breath of the house. Every day he stepped out to face danger, and every evening he returned with courage stitched into his tired smile. He showed us that fatherhood is not limited to one man. It can be shared, multiplied, and lived in silence.

One night, near the end of lockdown, we all sat together on the floor. The lights were dim. The fan turned lazily above us. No one was speaking much — but the silence wasn't heavy anymore. It was full. Full of memories, of gratitude, of unspoken promises. Pa, who still couldn't move his neck fully, whispered:

"The world outside has changed. But inside this house... we became unbreakable."

Tears filled my eyes because it was true.

We had been quarantined, yes. But never alone.

"Sometimes life locks the doors, not to punish you, but to protect you — so you discover that the greatest freedom isn't outside, but in the arms that never let you go."

That night, as I looked around the room — at my Pa lying on his bed but still smiling, at my Ma with tired yet fierce eyes, at Moty Ma adjusting her scarf over her surgical scar, at Mota Pa folding his arms quietly in the corner, at my siblings leaning against each other, and at my grandparents with folded hands in prayer — I realized something.

We didn't just survive the pandemic. We discovered the wealth that can never be stolen: family.

And as the world rushed back into its chaos, we carried forward a truth that will stay with us forever:

"We were never locked in. We were locked together. And in that, we found the greatest freedom of all."

Chapter 7

What the World Can Learn from Them

The hardest part of watching someone you love suffer isn't always the pain itself—it's watching how others respond to that pain. When my Pa had his accident, I learned the sharpest wound sometimes comes from people you once called friends. Those who once sat at our table, those who laughed with us, who claimed to be family—they disappeared. They did not visit. They did not call. Some, in fact, had taken advantage of Pa before his fall, using his goodness as a gateway for their gain. There were financial betrayals, unpaid debt, and promises that turned into silence. People he had stood by during their worst seasons suddenly forgot who he was in his.

I was young, and I'll be honest—it made me angry. I carried that anger like a shield. I wanted justice, I wanted truth to come out, and I wanted them to feel what we felt. But Pa never once said a harsh word about any of them. Not once. His response was something that took me years to understand—"It's okay. Money can be earned again. People... they come and go." It wasn't a weakness. It was a strength not to let betrayal change your heart.

That is what the world needs to see more of. We live in a culture that teaches revenge, that glorifies confrontation, that celebrates proving people wrong. But my Pa shows us a different path—a quieter, more dignified road. He taught us that when people break your trust, you don't have to break your character. That peace is more powerful than payback. Slowly, I learned to let go of the bitterness I once held for those so-called friends. Because I realised this—you cannot carry both anger and healing in the same heart. One will always make room for the other.

My father's silence wasn't defeat—it was a decision. A decision to not waste his energy on those who were never truly meant to stay. A decision to invest in what still mattered—family, recovery, and hope. That kind of forgiveness is not something the world often applauds, but it is something the world desperately needs.

We live in a time when loyalty is negotiable, and kindness is confused with naivety. But if the world could learn just one thing from Pa and Mota Pa, it would be this: Being good does not mean being foolish. It means choosing character over convenience, again and again.

There were no great speeches in our home. No lengthy sermons, no thundering declarations. And yet, every moment spent in the presence of Pa and Mota Pa was like being part of a living lesson—

one that wasn't taught in words but in quiet acts of discipline and compassion. Their lives became a daily classroom where silence was the teacher and example was the textbook.

Each morning, they woke early. Not because anyone asked them to. Not because there was applause waiting at the end of the day. But because they believed that responsibility is not a task—it is an identity. Their bodies often ached, silent stresses weighed down their minds, but they kept moving. They believed that when you have people depending on you, you don't wait for motivation—you become it.

There's something sacred about people who never make you feel like a burden—even when you know you are. That's the kind of safety the world is starving for. And that's exactly what they gave us: the ability to fall, without fear of being left behind.

The world often measures success by how high you rise, how far you go, and how loud your name is. But they taught us to measure success differently—by how kindly you live, how honestly you serve, and how gracefully you forgive. That is a currency far more lasting than fame or fortune.

Pa had every reason to turn bitter. Friends betrayed him. Life dealt him an unfair hand. His once-strong body was weakened by tragedy. But never—not once—did he let pain turn him cruel. In fact, I believe his compassion grew even more. He became softer, more patient, more understanding. Where others would have built walls, he built warmth. That is what the world can learn from him: don't let what breaks you make you unkind. Let it make you more human.

And then there's this—the art of showing up. Too often, people wait for the right time, the perfect words, the ideal situation to express love or offer help. But Pa and Mota Pa never waited. They showed up when it was messy, when they didn't know what to say, when they themselves struggled. They understood something very few do: presence heals more than advice ever will.

There were days when food was limited, when bills piled up like unanswered prayers, when we didn't know what tomorrow would bring. But there was laughter in our home. Not because life was easy, but because they protected our joy as if it were a fire they refused to let die. Even a shared cup of tea, even a late-night story under a fan that barely worked—they made it all feel magical. They believed happiness doesn't arrive when everything is perfect. It arrives when you decide that togetherness is more important than anything money can buy.

They also showed us how to stay gentle in a world that's constantly trying to harden you. How to keep your values steady, even when people around you are losing theirs. I remember once asking Mota Pa why he didn't confront someone who had insulted him. His answer was simple, but unforgettable: "I don't want to borrow their behaviour. I want to keep mine."

What a powerful idea—that we don't have to mirror the wrong we face. We can choose to be better. We can choose to be free.

Even their silence was instructive. When others would argue, they would pause. When they were in pain, they would sit quietly and still help others eat first. When tension filled the room, they would lower their voice instead of raising it. That restraint—that deep emotional control—is a lesson we rarely see in today's world, where shouting is mistaken for strength, and being loud is confused with being right.

In truth, they didn't just build a home. They built a culture—a culture of calm, of courage, of commitment. They taught us that sometimes, the most powerful thing you can do for your loved ones is simply to stay. Not solve everything. Don't say everything. Just stay. Keep showing up. Keep loving, quietly but completely.

So often, I think of how many people are walking through the world feeling empty, lost, angry—searching for meaning in places that can't offer it. And I want to tell them: come sit beside my Pa. Watch him bless food before eating. Watch him smile at a tired stranger. Watch how he carries pain without complaining, how he gives without waiting, how he loves without condition.

Because what the world can learn from them is not how to get ahead, but how to come home.

Even in their hardest seasons, Pa and Mota Pa never spoke like victims. Life had wounded them in ways only they knew—physically, financially, emotionally—and yet they refused to let those wounds define the way they walked. That's what made them different. Where others saw misfortune, they saw an opportunity to become stronger without becoming colder.

Every morning, before the chaos of life could knock at the door, they paused—even if just for a few seconds—to sit silently. I used to think it was simply tiredness. But now I know: it was surrender. A quiet conversation with life itself. They didn't call it meditation, but in their stillness, there was peace—the kind that says, "Whatever today brings, I will face it with grace."

They believed that discipline wasn't something you showed to the world. It was something you owed to yourself. Mota Pa never skipped a single medicine, not even on days when his body ached too much to move. Pa did his daily exercises, not for anyone's applause, but as a duty to his soul. They never postponed what needed to be done. They never waited for the "right day" to begin again. That is another lesson the world must learn: there is no perfect time to start healing, rebuilding, forgiving—there is only now.

I remember once asking Pa, "How do you keep going when everything feels broken?" He smiled—a tired but steady smile—and said, "Because even a broken clock shows the right time twice a day. So don't stop. You are still useful. You are still worthy."

What was the magic in his thinking? He didn't need the world to tell him he mattered. He decided that he did. And that is where real power begins.

In a society that glorifies busyness, they honoured stillness. They understood that silence wasn't emptiness—it was where life breathed. In their pauses, in the quiet way they folded clothes, in the way they lit a lamp before eating, the world could learn how to slow down. How to treat small, ordinary things like sacred rituals. The world rushes through meals, conversations, and even emotions. But they moved as if time were their friend, not their enemy.

And through all this, they never lost their humour. Even with sugar problems, back pain, stress, and unpaid bills, they found a way to laugh. I remember once, Pa couldn't sit straight after a painful week, but when I asked him how he felt, he chuckled, "My spine may be tired, but my spirit still dances."

That's what kept our family alive—laughter that was born not from ease, but from endurance.

They were the kind of men who believed in fixing what could be fixed and accepting what could not. When the pressure was high, they didn't lash out. They adjusted their minds, not just their plans. They understood a truth many people overlook: life won't always get easier, but you can always grow stronger.

There's also something else the world must learn from them—contentment. To smile at what you have, even when it is less than what you once had. Pa never envied rich men. He never spoke badly of people who had more. His heart was never hungry for status—only for stability, safety, and peace. And Mota Pa? He never complained when others rested while he worked. He simply carried on, because the family needed him to.

If you truly watch them, you'll see that emotional intelligence is not about speaking clever words. It's about knowing when silence is enough. Knowing when to forgive. Knowing when to stay, even when walking away feels easier. These lessons are not written in books, not studied in schools—they are born from pain, polished by patience, and proven in presence.

They didn't just survive life—they gave it meaning not only for themselves, but for all of us. They reminded us that strength is not how hard your hands are, but how soft your heart remains after it has been hurt. That faith is not about praying for miracles, but about continuing even when miracles don't come.

The more I grow, the more I understand—we weren't raised by instructions. Examples raised us. There were no lectures, no textbooks on kindness. Just two men who lived their values so faithfully that they became the blueprint for our lives.

They didn't just love us—they carried us. Not once or twice, but every single day, even when their own backs ached and their hearts were heavy. They taught us that true influence is not about words spoken in public, but about actions repeated in private.

I often think about how children copy what they see. Most kids I knew copied their favourite superheroes. We copied Pa and Mota Pa. Their gestures became ours—the way they offered the first bite of food to someone else, the way they never wasted water, the way they said "thank you" even for the smallest kindness.

And I've realised—this is exactly what the world is starving for. We have endless motivational speeches, self-help books, and videos that promise to change your life in ten steps. But none of them compares to the quiet consistency of people like Pa and Mota Pa.

"A good heart may be silent, but it echoes in every life it touches."

Their silence was not emptiness—it was depth. It wasn't weakness—it was wisdom. And that silence still speaks to me today.

They never defined strength with words. They let strength define itself through them. It wasn't about muscles or dominance. It was about rising early when their bodies were tired. About giving without expecting. About smiling even when their world was falling apart inside.

The world today measures everything—calories, steps, likes, income. But they measured only one thing: whether they had done enough good with the day given to them. And because of that, even when they went to bed exhausted, they slept in peace.

In a time when success is measured by fame and fortune, they lived by a different compass. Some people chase recognition—they chase meaning. Some people collect things—they collect people. Their worth was not in what they owned. It was in what they gave. And even when their hands were empty, their hearts remained full.

When life gave them little, they created enough. Enough food to share. Enough peace to sleep. Enough faith to survive. Watching them, I learned that peace is not found in abundance, but in gratitude.

"Quiet consistency is louder than empty promises."

Their consistency built our home. It built our courage. It built our story. And now, it stands as a lesson for the world.

If you're reading this with a heart that feels tired or used, I want to remind you—your value isn't decided by who stays. It's revealed by how you rise when others walk away. The world may not always return your love. But that doesn't make your love any less worthy.

"When people show you their absence, let it teach you presence."

Pa and Mota Pa lived this truth without ever spelling it out. They never forced anyone to stay in their life. They never begged for loyalty or chased after those who walked away. Instead, they poured their love into the ones who chose to remain. That is something the world desperately needs to learn: not everyone is meant to finish the journey with you, but those who do—those are the ones worth building your life around.

Your softness is not a flaw. It's your quiet rebellion against a world that hardens too easily. Pa showed us that gentleness has more power than aggression. Mota Pa proved that patience can move mountains that anger never will. They both reminded us that kindness is not weakness—it is a force that outlives betrayal, disappointment, and even loss.

Keep being good. Keep being kind. The world may overlook you now, but souls like yours build legacies that never die. The true builders of history are not always the ones with statues or headlines. Sometimes, they are the men who sit silently at a sick brother's bedside for months, or the women who cook meals through their own pain just to keep hope alive.

And if you're looking for that spark—that reason to keep going—don't search the skies. Look around you. Look at the people you love. Look at the person you are becoming. Your purpose isn't a prize waiting at the finish line. It's a choice you make every day—to show up, to try again, to offer your heart even when it is bruised.

"Start again. Not because you failed—but because you've grown."

Pa and Mota Pa never chased trophies. They never needed the world's applause. What they built was far greater: they became people others could lean on. That is the greatest success of all—to be someone whose presence brings calm, whose strength is quiet, and whose love outlasts the storm.

So, if you're holding on to grief, to anger, to betrayal—you don't have to keep it. Let it go, not for them, but for you. Free yourself from the story that hurt you, and write one that heals you.

"Even if no one claps for your resilience, let it echo inside your own heart."

You are not behind—you are becoming. And every time you choose love over revenge, calm over chaos, forgiveness over fury—you become more like the people the world forgets to celebrate but so desperately needs.

And maybe, that is the greatest lesson of all: greatness is not in being remembered by the world—it is in being remembered by the ones who sit at your table, who carry your name, who whisper your values into the ears of the next generation.

When I look at Pa and Mota Pa today, I don't just see two men who carried their family. I see two teachers the world never knew it had. Teachers of patience, of sacrifice, of quiet strength. Their classroom was our home. Their lessons were lived, not spoken. And their students—us—carry their syllabus in our hearts forever.

If the world ever asks me what true success looks like, I will not point to wealth, or power, or fame. I will point to two brothers who chose each other again and again, even when life gave them every reason to walk away.

And one day, when I am asked what the world can learn from them, I will say this:

"The world does not need more heroes in capes. It needs more brothers who hold each other's hands in the storm. It needs more families who choose love over ego. It needs more people who believe that being good is enough. Because goodness, when practised long enough, becomes the kind of legacy even time cannot erase."

And with that, I close this chapter—knowing it is not just a story about my Pa and Mota Pa. It is a mirror held to the world. A mirror that whispers: this is who you could be, if only you choose love the way they did.

Chapter 8

The Fire Within Us: A Guide to Resilience and Hope

"The world sees strong people and assumes they were born that way. But strength is often stitched in silence – sewn from pain, illness, sacrifice, and the fire that never lets us give up."

There are two kinds of battles in life- the ones the world sees, and the ones we fight quietly every day, when no one is watching.

My father? He lived with new pain every single day. Some days it was physical, some days emotional, and some days invisible, but he never showed it. He just smiled a little and carried on as if pain had no permission to step on him.

My mother sacrificed everything. Her youth, her dreams, her health. She lived for us. For the family. And yet, she never demanded anything in return. Her silence was nobility, her patience, her power.

Moty ma- she fought her private war, pregnancy struggle, a battle with breast cancer, and later, battles with high blood pressure and diabetes, but if you asked her how she was, she'd always say, "I am good". She never let her suffering dim her smile; that was her rebellion against fate.

And Mota pa, the spine of our entire family- his pressure would rise with stress, but not once did he step back from responsibilities. Even when his hands trembled, he held us up. Even when his heart ached, he stayed steady for everyone else.

Every person in my home had their own war, and yet, we never collapsed. Because when one person is bent, the others become the support. That is what a real family looks like- not perfect people, but people who choose each other again and again, no matter the pain.

"The strength of family isn't measured by smiles in photographs, but by tears wiped away in silence, by hands that hold when no one is watching. "

Many people ask, "How do we find that fire? How do we get that kind of strength?"

It's hidden in small daily habits. It's in the choices you make when no one is clapping for you. When you wake up tired but still cook for your children, when you go to work with a headache just so the house can run, when you smile, even though you're breaking inside.

That's the fire.

How to build a fire within you?

1. Find a reason bigger than yourself: if you're only living for yourself, your motivation will break when life hits you. But if you live for your mother's smile, your child's future, your father's peace- that's when the fire becomes unstoppable.

2. Stop waiting for the right time: pain will always be there. Conditions will never be perfect. Start now. The spark doesn't wait. It's created when you take the first step- with fear, with doubt, with trembling hands.

3. Create rituals, not routine: routine becomes boring. Rituals have meaning. Say a prayer before you leave work. Have a coffee with someone you love every evening. Turn actions into love.

4. Learn to fall in love with effort, not outcome: some days your best work will go unnoticed. Still, do it. Because when your reason is love, results don't matter.

"Sometimes the fire inside you doesn't roar. Sometimes it whispers, Try again tomorrow.' That whisper is enough."

There were many nights we didn't know how we'd survive. Medicines were expensive. Food had to be stretched. Hope had to be created from scratch.

But then, someone would crack a joke, and someone would fry some extra chips. Someone would say, "Let's watch a movie together tonight." And that one moment of togetherness would create enough spark to carry us through another week.

The spark doesn't come from outside. It comes from within- when you choose love over bitterness.

When you choose effort over excuse. When you choose to keep going, even when no one is clapping.

"The 5 minutes of fire" Rule:

- 1 minute: deep breathing and inhaling the new day.
- 1 minute: Gratitude- say 3 things you're thankful for.
- 1 minute: physical movement- even a stretch.
- 1 minute: affirmation- say out loud. "I will not give up today."
- 1 minute: do one small thing for someone else.

5 minutes. That's all it takes to begin the fire.

"You don't need a hundred steps to change your life. Sometimes, you just need five- done with love, done every day."

No one was perfect. But everyone was present. That's what kept us burning.

"It is not the absence of pain that makes you strong, but the presence of purpose in the middle of the pain."

Sometimes people say, "I feel stuck. I don't know what my goal is. How can I live with fire?"

Here's a truth you might not want to hear: You don't need a "big dream" to live a meaningful life. You just need small purposes to live with intensity.

Try this:

- Make someone laugh every day.
- Help your parents without being asked.
- Learn one thing every day that your future self will thank you for.
- Choose not to argue even when you can win.
- Call someone who misses you.

These are not small actions- they are sparks, and sparks light fire.

One evening, I found my father sitting quietly. His body was stiff, drained by days of endless efforts. I asked him, "Pa, don't you feel tired of being strong?"

He smiled at me and said, "I don't have the option to get tired, because if I fall, who will rise for you?"

That was his fire.

"Real warriors don't choose strength; they are chosen by the people who depend on them."

Try living one week using this simple "3C Rule".

1. Clarity: Every morning, ask yourself, "What is one thing I want to feel proud of tonight?"
2. Courage: do one thing that scares you. A hard phone call, speaking up, trying something you.
3. Compassion: Be gentle with yourself and others. Speak kindly. Listen more, judge less.

Keep a journal. Track your days. See how your soul begins to light up.

"You won't always feel brave, but you can always choose to be gentle. - with yourself, with your pain, and with your path."

We didn't have vacations or luxuries or fancy hobbies; what we had was each other, and that was enough.

Sometimes our fire came from laughing during dinner. Sometimes it came from sitting silently beside each other on the balcony. Sometimes it came from watching our grandparents sip tea, their hands trembling, but their eyes full of peace.

Even now, when I feel lost, I don't think of success. I think of those moments, which were the fire that built me.

"You don't have to chase the sun. Sometimes sitting near the candle in a quiet room can remind you of your light."

There will be days when the fire feels like ash. Days when nothing makes sense. When your body feels heavy. When the thought of continuing seems exhausting.

It's okay.

The fire doesn't lie.

It just hides beneath the weight.

And in those moments, you don't need to roar.

You just need to breathe.

You just need to rest.

You just need to survive for an hour.

Then- do one kind thing. Call someone. Cry if needed. That's enough to keep the fire alive.

"The fire within you is not a flame to show others- it's a warmth to keep yourself going."

Pain teaches what comfort can't.

It teaches how to see people clearly- beyond what they show. It teaches how to love without conditions- when someone is no longer strong, beautiful, or useful. It teaches how to keep going- not because you are fearless, but because someone else depends on your courage.

My pa never taught me how to fight. He just showed me what it looked like- when he couldn't stand with swollen knees and a half-broken back. My mota pa never lectured on leadership. He just carried a family of nine through a pandemic, paralysis, a cancer battle, and poverty- without raising his voice.

Every loss in life- whether health, hope, or happiness- creates an empty space. But emptiness is also an opportunity.

Use that space:

- To plant a new habit.
- To write a letter you never had time for.
- To reconnect with your inner child.
- To pray, even if you don't believe- just to feel something greater than your pain.

In our family, loss came in layers- health, finances, freedom. But with each loss, we added something:

- More time together.
- More storytelling over tea.
- More gratitude for what remained.

That's how the fire grows- not in what's taken, but in what's added after.

"Every loss leaves you with two choices: light a candle or curse the dark. Light it every time, even if your hands shake."

In life, we don't always meet angels with wings. Sometimes, we meet them in buses. In hospital waiting rooms, or inside homes where every person is tired, but still fighting for each other.

I once met a stranger at the medical store. I was buying medicine for my Pa and Moty Ma. My hands were shaking not from the weight of bags, but the bills, the fear, the pressure of being strong for everyone.

He looked at me and asked gently," Are you okay?"

I nodded, but he saw through me. He said something that changed me forever: "Sometimes, God gives the hardest paths to those who carry the softest heart. Don't harden. Just burn brighter."

If you are reading this and feeling lost, let this chapter hold your hand.

Let it remind you that you do not need to roar to be powerful.

You do not need to win to be worthy.

You do not need to shine to be enough.

Just keep the fire alive — even if today, it is only a spark.

Because one day, when you least expect it,

that spark will rise,

Your heart will open again,

and you will realise that every silent battle, every setback, every night you cried quietly...

was shaping a version of you that didn't just survive — but transformed.

And when you reach that moment, you will whisper the truth my family lived every day:

"I am still here.

I am still trying.

And that is enough to set my world on fire again."

Chapter 9

Childhood Interrupted, Adulthood Learned Early

"Some children are given toys to carry; others are given responsibilities. Some are handed balloons; others are handed burdens. But even in the weight, there is a strange kind of strength waiting to be born."

Our story was never about a perfect childhood. It was about a childhood interrupted — cut short by circumstances we never asked for, tested by situations we never deserved. When my father's accident paralysed him, our lives shifted overnight. The home that once echoed with carefree laughter now carried whispers of worry, unpaid bills, medicines stacked on shelves, and unspoken fears that even children could not ignore.

We were young, too young, to be exposed to life's harshness. Yet we heard things no child should ever hear. People who didn't understand — or perhaps chose not to — made comments that stung like arrows. Whispers about our father's condition. Questions about how we would survive. Pity disguised as sympathy. Each word was a reminder of the storm we were forced to grow up in. My brother, my sister, and I carried those wounds silently because there was no one to hand them back to.

The world rarely notices how children change when life throws storms too early. We were expected to play, but instead we learned to plan. We should have been carefree, but instead we carried care itself.

My brother and sister, especially, became mirrors of Pa and Mota Pa. They were still so young, yet I saw them standing like pillars in moments where even adults might have faltered. My brother, with hands still too small to lift heavy weights, learned to take on responsibilities far bigger than himself. He was the one who held Pa's head gently when feeding time came. He was the one who fetched medicines, ran errands, and stood in lines that should have been for grown men. His childhood was measured not in toys, but in tasks.

My sister, too, transformed in silence. She became the soft strength of the house — the one who prayed aloud when the rest of us kept our fears hidden. She stayed awake at night to check on Pa's breathing, slipping into the room like a guardian angel. Sometimes she'd whisper promises to God: "Please keep him safe. I'll do better. I'll be stronger." She carried burdens not on her back, but in her heart.

And me? I was sixteen, but I felt decades older. I learned to calculate bills, read prescriptions, and make decisions that should never fall on a teenager's shoulders. There was no space for teenage dreams or distractions. My "classroom" was life itself, and my "exams" were daily survival.

Together, the three of us formed a shield around our parents. Not perfectly, not always bravely — but wholeheartedly. We became, in our own ways, the second generation of strength. What Pa and Mota Pa had once done for the family, we now began to imitate — clumsy at first, but growing steadier with every trial.

It was as if life was preparing us for something greater. Parenting itself seemed to arrive early for us — not in raising children, but in raising responsibilities. And though it hurt, it also taught us that everything in life truly comes at the right time, even if the timing feels unfair.

Sometimes I wondered what life might have been like if that one accident had never happened. Suppose Pa had never left home that morning on September 7, 2014. If he had returned the same strong man he always was. Perhaps our house would have been different. Perhaps our childhood would have been filled with fewer responsibilities and more ordinary dreams. Perhaps our financial life would have been smoother, freer, and more comfortable.

But then another thought always arrived, like a calming hand on my shoulder — at least he is still with us. At least we can still hear his voice, see his smile, and feel his presence. That realisation shifted everything. What could have been a curse became a strange kind of blessing. We were not robbed of a father; we were given the chance to love him more deeply than most children ever do.

Money was tight, yes. Dreams often felt postponed. But our hearts were still full — because Pa was alive. And sometimes, survival itself is the greatest blessing you can count.

It was in those moments that gratitude quietly replaced grief. We learned that it was better to count what remained than to mourn what was lost.

As the years passed, something remarkable began to unfold. My brother and sister, I often look at them now and think: if they can hold our family at such a young age, imagine what kind of giants they will become as adults. They've already proven that strength is not about muscles, but about carrying love with both hands.

And I realised something else too — parenting always arrives on time. Life may not give you the father who runs beside you at the park, but it may give you a brother who stands like a shield. It may not give you a mother who can rest, but it may give you a sister who becomes her second heartbeat. Somehow, life always provides — not in the way you expect, but in the way you need.

Our story is proof.

We listened to words we never deserved, endured judgments we should never have faced. People looked at us differently because our father was paralysed. Some whispered. Some doubted. Some pitied. Those words cut deeper than any financial struggle. But still — we stood. We stood because Pa was still with us. His breath, his voice, his smile — even in pain — were blessings bigger than anything we had lost.

And maybe that's the greatest truth we discovered: when you are stripped of what the world calls "normal," you begin to see what truly matters. We had no luxury, no freedom from hardship, but we had Pa alive, and that alone was wealth beyond measure.

Now, when I look at my brother and sister, I see a fire that life itself lit. They have grown into young souls who can hold an entire family on their shoulders, the way Pa and Mota Pa once did. They are the proof that struggle is not the end of innocence — it is the beginning of strength.

And me? I carry it all in my heart —the stolen ease, but also the gift of knowing that even in the harshest storms, we were never truly abandoned.

Because in the end, our story is not about what we lost. It is about what we became.

We became children who turned into warriors.

We became siblings who turned into pillars.

We became a family that turned wounds into wisdom.

And maybe, just maybe, that is what the world needs to learn: sometimes the hardest childhoods create the strongest legacies.

Even today, as I sit far away in the United States, every breath of mine still feels tied to theirs. I may live oceans apart, but my heart beats in rhythm with my family. Every morning here begins with the thought of them, and every night ends with gratitude that they are holding each other the way Pa and Mota Pa once held us all.

They are financially independent now. My brother has built a business from scratch while also carrying forward Pa's catering business — not just as a livelihood, but as a legacy. My sister has grown into a brave soul, someone who can shoulder responsibilities with quiet strength. And my mother, still the backbone, keeps us all connected no matter where I am in the world.

To be honest, none of this has been easy. Behind every smile lies sacrifice. Behind every success lies sleepless nights. Yet, they've shown me — and can show the world — that no matter how heavy life becomes, you must never let go of each other's hands.

What everyone can learn from our story is this: don't let your hardships make you bitter. Don't let circumstances divide you. Every day is an opportunity — to hold your family tighter, to remind each other that at the end of every storm, the only shelter you will ever truly have been the people who love you.

And above all, believe. Believe in your family. Believe in their strength when yours is gone. Believe in the power of togetherness when everything else fails. Because the truth is simple yet eternal: the world may forget you, friends may abandon you, wealth may vanish — but family will always remain.

That is our legacy. That is our inheritance. And that is our unshakable truth.

Epilogue: And So, We Continue...

As I place the final period on this book, I realise something: stories never really end. They live on in the way we carry them, in the way they change us.

My family's journey has been one of floods, accidents, sickness, betrayals, and endless trials. But it has also been a journey of prayers, laughter, survival, and love that refused to let go.

If you take only one lesson from these pages, let it be this: family is not defined by comfort — it is defined by commitment. When the world falls apart, you don't need riches, status, or applause. You just need each other.

And when you have that, you have everything.

So, to you — dear reader — I leave this final thought:

When life tests you, don't ask "why me?" Ask instead, "Who can I hold onto, and who can I hold up?" Because at the end of every storm, the only shelter that lasts is love.

Our story is done on paper — but in life, it continues. In every prayer whispered, in every meal shared, in every sacrifice made quietly and without recognition.

And maybe, just maybe, when you close this book, you will open your arms a little wider to your own family. Because of that, more than anything, is the true legacy we hoped to leave behind.

Acknowledgments

This book is not mine alone — it belongs to every soul who walked beside us when life tried to bring us to our knees.

To my family — Pa, Mota Pa, Ma, Moty Ma, my brother, my sister, and my grandparents — you are the heartbeat of every page. Your love, your sacrifices, your laughter through tears are the reason these words exist at all.

To my extended family — my mother's sisters, my father's cousins, and every relative who stepped forward in our darkest nights — thank you for proving that love has no conditions. You reminded me that family is not just who you are born to, but who shows up when the storms come.

And to every reader holding this book — thank you. Thank you for stepping into our home, sitting with our pain, and celebrating our hope. If these chapters remind you to hold your people closer, to forgive faster, and to love without hesitation — then this book has done its work.

About the Author

Hinali Dudhane is a Civil Engineer whose life and values have been shaped by discipline, resilience, and a deep commitment to family. Originally from India, she is now building her career in the United States and balances technical expertise with a grounded sense of responsibility and empathy.

Her professional journey reflects precision and determination, while her personal experiences have strengthened her belief in unity, integrity, and emotional courage. These principles guide her work both inside and outside her field.

Two Shadows, One Light is her first book, born from a desire to preserve the legacy of the two men who defined the meaning of unconditional support in her life. Through this work, she aims to offer readers clarity, comfort, and a renewed understanding of family strength.

With this debut, Hinali begins a writing path she intends to continue, creating meaningful work that uplifts, inspires, and honours the values she lives by.

Author's Note

Some books are written with ink. This one is written with bloodline, sacrifice and the quiet courage of two brothers who held the sky above an entire family – so the rest of us could stand.

I didn't write this story as a writer. I wrote it as a daughter. A witness. Someone who watched two ordinary men live extraordinary lives, and my heart couldn't carry everything anymore- not without putting it somewhere safe. And for me, the safest place was paper.

This book holds no fiction, no filters; it holds the weight of a family that bent but never broke. My Pa, who lost the use of his legs but never the fire in his spirit. My Mota Pa, who became the roof under which all of us survived. And me, the girl who carried it all in her heart until it poured out as pages.

I started this book in the United States, where I moved for a master's degree. Today, I work as a civil engineer- a new world, a new chapter. But my roots, my foundation- that will always be them.

If this book has touched your heart, I want you to know- my story doesn't end here. I have lived a beautiful journey. If life allows, I'll write a second book. A new season. New lessons. More of the magic that shaped me.

But for now, this is where I leave you.

With gratitude.

With tears.

With the memory of two men who didn't just raise a family...

They held the sky.

With all my heart,

Hinali Dudhane

(Daughter of two pillars)

❏ ❏ ❏